Take This Child

by
Calley Harrell Reed

Take This Child

Does God still speak?

One family follows God's supernatural trail all the way to an orphan waiting in the heart of the Amazon.

ISBN-13: 978-1484999707
ISBN-10: 1484999703

First printing 2013
Printed in the United States of America

The names of the individuals in this story have been changed to protect their identity. The scriptural references have been taken from various translations of the Bible. The Books and Authors mentioned in this book do not constitute their agreement or support of the content of this book.

It is the expressed desire of the author to allow this book to be reproduced in any form with the understanding that the author's proceeds from the sale of this book go to support Abundant Life Ministries to Peru. Also that any quotations would not be taken out of context and all would be for the Glory of the Lord, Jesus Christ.

Published with the help of Firestarter Publications
120 Glade Place, Dover, Arkansas 72837, firestarterpublications.com

Contents

Preface

There I sat in a canoe, in the middle of a fast moving, muddy river. Both sides of the murky river were lined with thick green vegetation. South America. How did I get here? I sat in my canoe alone and completely terrified. It was what I immediately saw around me that scared me the most. I was encircled by dying people who were fighting to stay afloat in the river. The people screamed for my help. They raised their arms toward me, hollering and shrieking as the current pulled them along. They were not in a canoe. They were struggling in the river and snakes swam between them. Their cries were stiffening.

My fear did not come from the snakes, the current, or my being alone. I was overwhelmed with the responsibility upon me. It was a selfish fear. I knew these people needed help, but my anxiety kept me from responding. I was strangely convinced that if I let someone into my boat, they would only throw me out. I sat paralyzed in my own anxieties. Who are these people? Why me? Why?

I rationalized over and over in my mind all of the reasons why I couldn't possibly rescue anyone. After all, only one, or maybe two people could fit into my canoe. There seemed to be hundreds fighting for life all around me. "I am weak," I thought. I don't know these tan skinned, dark haired people.

It was settled. There was too great of a risk for me to help anyone. What difference could helping one or two of these desperate people make? After I made up my mind, I grabbed my paddles. With several forceful pushes, I paddled away from all of the cries of despair. They became more and more distant until they finally disappeared into nothing. I couldn't hear the screaming. I could no longer see the hurting dark faces, and the large black eyes expecting me to do something to change their certain death.

They were gone. They were all gone.

As I turned around a bend in the river, the water suddenly turned into a still calm. My canoe seemed to guide itself to the bank, where I stepped out onto a grassy slope. Up ahead stood a large shopping mall in all of its American glory. I trudged toward it and my mind decidedly shrugged away all that I had just taken in. My agenda turned to going inside and shopping the sales.

I woke up....my forehead was covered in sweat, and large desperate breaths caused my chest to heave up and down. I was back in reality. Thankfulness that I was comfortably sleeping in my bed overwhelmed me to tears. It was only a dream. It was only a dream. No reason to be burdened. All is well. The reassuring thoughts were a sad attempt to keep me from owning up to the scene I had just witnessed while in a deep sleep. I knew I had just had a God dream.

Chapter 1

Surrender

I have never been a big dreamer (while sleeping, anyway). A handful of times, I believe God has spoken to me in my dreams. Only a couple of times, have I had such a vivid dream, that I awoke with the knowledge the dream would be there with me for life. A perfect picture, with even distinct colors, forever etched into my brain...branded there to stay.

What was God trying to show me? What was it in my life that would keep me from rescuing people? I considered myself to be completely surrendered to whatever the Lord would call me to do. The dream made me wonder how God considered me.

One thing was certain. I, the pastor's wife, the worship leader- could hear plainly before me, "You let go of your fears, and I will use you and your family in ways you never imagined possible." What were my fears?

Little did I know, our family was about to see so many aspects of this dream played out. We were going to be called to go beyond ourselves into a walk of faith that would stretch us immeasurably more than we had ever experienced before.

By anyone's view, our hands and lives were full. We were blessed, and we were happy. Our idea of wealth since being married and having kids had never equated to what our world called wealthy, but we felt our cup was running over with good things- good things that kept us moving. Danny and I had been married for 8 years. We had three children, all boys. We were far from rich, financially speaking. Our double wide trailer was situated on a plot of land in the middle of a small town in Louisiana. It was sort of an island of land in the city- I considered it the best of both worlds. Private and convenient. Our home suited our family perfectly, and most of the things that filled it were given to us, or were old and reupholstered. Looking around our home, we could see so many ways God had provided and blessed our family. We had two running vehicles, both paid off. With much budgeting and planning, we were able to take yearly road trips all over the country and an occasional trip to the beach with our boys. We were surrounded by family and friends, and our church was a place of joy and refuge that was continually growing and thriving. We had extra money to do fun things with our kids on the weekends, all while still being able to give to others in need. What more could we ask for- and also, what more could we commit to?

Josiah was our energetic and creative five year old, and Isaac, our three-year-old outdoorsman. Amaus was our laid back, nursing toddler. Danny worked a full-time job as part owner of an independent insurance agency and had recently become the senior pastor of the small church where he had served as youth pastor for about 10 years. Danny and I, as a team, were eager to see souls saved and to see the broken find hope and healing. Danny (by his unbiased wife's standards) was a devoted hands-on father who was constantly striving to spend the little extra time he had wisely for the kingdom of God. I also stayed busy teaching an adult bible study, Sunday school, and serving as a worship leader at our church, in addition to home schooling our two oldest sons. I was able to further pour out myself through my newly evolved passion of being a birth doula, which gave me the opportunity to support and coach women giving birth.

Like any mom, I had days that were seemingly smooth and easy, and others when I wondered what else might possibly go wrong; days when I felt I might go bonkers! Picture walking through a house with speed while Cheerios (ie: Honey Nut Rings, or possibly Cocoa "Rocks," no pun intended) crunch beneath your toes, due to an entire box being poured onto the living room floor. All this as you're on your way to breaking up the throw pillow Gladiators that is taking place in the kitchen. You pass by the back bathroom where the toilet is overflowing because of a son who likes to use an entire roll of toilet paper at each bathroom stop. This is a good picture of day-to-day events in the Reed house. My response to days like this varied. With enough sleep and God's grace, I could handle situations like these with ease, and then sometimes I felt like calling a game of "hide and seek" and going to hibernate in the bathtub with a blanket pulled over my head, while the kids searched for a bit. Even on those hard days though, I knew our lives were abundantly blessed by the Savior. I was right where I wanted to be, doing exactly what I wanted to be doing. I had long ago laid down my own selfish ambitions and plans and embraced with joy what I knew the Lord had called me to do. I could have never imagined what adventure and delight lay in being a homemaker, a mother, and a wife. When I had been in college only 8 years before, pursuing my dream opera career, God had quietly disrupted my good intentions and revealed what He had created me especially for. There had been no looking back, and no disappointment in the path I had surrendered to.

Our lives were stacked to the brim with things we loved, but stacked nonetheless. Any extra time we had, we spent in outreach with our church or enjoying the little leisure time remaining with extended family. Top that with regular household needs and a few eccentric chores we chose to add to our daily regimen (cow milking, chicken feeding and gardening), and we could easily, as most of mankind, classify ourselves as too busy doing God's work to respond to any further call.

From time to time, my thoughts wandered back to the dream that I had experienced a year before. I shared it with our Wednesday Bible study group during a discussion on surrender. God had definitely burdened me about my level of surrender through it, if nothing else. I often thought of the thick vegetation lining the muddy river. I thought of the tanned faces asking me of all people for help. Why had I dreamed of this place I had never been? During that year of thinking, I had two more dreams of being in South America. There was nothing else inherently flamboyant about the subsequent dreams. I was just there in South America, along with Danny, our kids, and my dad and step-mom.

Life continued on its normal pattern for me, striving to walk in the presence of God. Striving to begin each day in His Word and ending each day with thanksgiving, even when things may have gotten a little hairy during the hours in between. His grace is always sufficient. Life moved forward. Homeschooling, teaching the boys...one day ran into another, and one season ran into the next.

But just like the surprise cold fronts that sometimes cut into our mild Louisiana autumns, my life was totally interrupted out of nowhere one morning. I woke up with a passion burning in my heart. A passion that I had not thought of in several years...

Chapter 2

Adoption

It wasn't a new thought for us. Danny and I had prayed about adoption when Isaac, our second child, had been about a year old. It, no doubt, seemed like an impossible feat at the time. I called agencies and asked numerous questions, and I still received mostly the same answers. Our family just did not have the income required for international or domestic adoption, especially since we had two small children in our household. We looked into fostering children who were more likely to need permanent homes, but were discouraged by a state social worker from the foster system, if adoption was our intent. We were told that the primary goal in fostering was for the parents of the fostered children to be rehabilitated and the children brought home to their biological parents. We assumed that adoption just might not be possible for us. The thought had not been brought up to discussion point between Danny and me since that time. We had put the idea on the shelf. After all, what else could we do? We could only assume that either adoption wasn't God's plan for us, or our timing was off somehow.

That morning though, when I arose from bed, there was no question about what I was hearing. It was a heart wrenching, piercing cry cutting to my very core; ringing so loudly with desperation, I could not possibly paddle away. I was not in a dream. This loud multitude that rang the fiber of everything in me would not be ignored any longer. I could not cast aside what I knew to be the very heart of God, now burning within myself. It wasn't one of my children that had awakened me that morning before the sun came up. It was clearly the cry of the fatherless that quaked through my schedules, through my to-do list...through my selfishness. That same-o, typical busy day of schooling, cooking, cleaning, and diaper washing had been interrupted with a beckoning from the Holy Spirit.

I sat aside some less important tasks in response to the heavy burden I now felt was mine and began emailing ministries and agencies immediately. The presence of the Lord was urging me forward in this purpose all the while. I was surely caught up in what felt to be an urgency.

When I thought about these obvious facts, I questioned my sanity. Our finances weren't much different from the first time we had looked into adopting. Our children, well...there were more of them now! My mind told me over and over again that I was pursuing a pointless cause and would surely be shot down. The Spirit of God kept urging me onward.

The next morning I continued researching, taking each available moment to see what I could discover. Was there an agency that would accept us? What would people think about a family with three small children, and especially a one-and-a-half year old, desiring to adopt more children? What would Danny think, as I had yet to bring up the discussion with him? The previous evening had not given me a window to bring up the topic. He had been busy with something, and for some reason, we had not had a time for me to sit down and unload this burden I was carrying.

That afternoon, on the second day of my research and internal struggle, the perfect opportunity arose. Danny had to bring some cows to sell at market, and we had a good two hour ride ahead of us. Driving to the sale barn was something I always looked forward to. It was a wonderful chance to relax and visit. That day in particular, I had something that I was dying to discuss. On the way home, as we pulled the old, now empty trailer behind us, and the kids napped in their car seats, I finally brought up what had been so heavy upon me for two days.

"Danny," I told him, as I reasoned the best way to approach the topic of more children, after an extremely trying day of mothering.

"Do you ever think about adoption anymore?"

That was about all I could muster up. Simple, and to the point. There was a little pause, if I remember correctly. There had to have been because I had already, in that small space of silence, become sure that Danny was thinking I was absolutely nuts. I knew it. Danny was rewinding the last week of our hectic lives, and the most recent behavioral issues with our kids. Yep. He was configuring how to explain to me that I must be needing a little more sleep at night. I had officially lost it.

These assumptions about my husband's thoughts were probably rooted in many conversations we had had over the last year. Danny and I both had admitted that we felt doubts about our own personal trust in the Lord in dealing with the size of our family. If we really trusted God as the giver of life, then why did we feel the need to control or plan that part of our lives based on what we felt comfortable with? No biological child was going to accidentally be created that God had not planned before one of its days came to be. It was easy to say, "I don't believe I'm supposed to have any more children." But something in us also said that if that belief were true, then we surely wouldn't have to work in order to prevent another child from coming to be . Satan wasn't going to give us a baby, for crying out loud. We knew God alone was the giver of life, and He calls children a blessing.

But these conversations were always left unsettled. They ended open. There was, honestly, never any real resolve or surrender on either of our parts. We couldn't picture ourselves as a Duggar/ Cheaper by the Dozen, kind of family. The thought pretty much scared me. I knew I couldn't base my calling on my capabilities, and I knew my rationale didn't add up to faith. But we seemed to search for a loophole in this struggle, never really finding rest. So now, with another conversation on adding children to our home, what would his response be?

Danny's answer still rings in my heart. He looked at me briefly with both a shocked and amused look on his face.

"Calley!" Danny seemed shocked, as he went on. "Yesterday and today, I've been online in my spare time at work, researching how it would be possible for us to go about adopting..."

I stammered, "Wha, what do you mean?!"

"Well, I've been researching how in the world it could be possible for us to adopt- the means of going about it."

The silence that followed next was way more satisfying than the first. Tears filled my eyes to the brim and streamed down my face, blurring the passing buildings and fields.

We were both overwhelmed with the goodness of God and the joy of knowing His hand was moving in our lives. We both had been hit with the same burden without ever discussing it. Jesus was directing our lives, and we both knew it. God had burdened both of our hearts on the same two days. What a strange and beautiful confirmation!

My thoughts quickly went to my dream of surrender in South America. Something in me knew there was some sort of connection. All at once, I blurted out the river of feelings and emotions I had. I reminded him of the dream. Danny and I both relished in the wonder of what God could be up to. We both rode down the road in awe of the hand of the Lord so clearly directing us. What was God doing in us? It was as if He had handed us a small piece of a puzzle. What would the big picture turn out to be? We felt an assurance that Jesus was the master artist in whatever was going on, and that whatever He was doing in us would far surpass our own short-sighted plans.

Chapter 3

Immovable

Before too long, Danny and I finally had the courage to make a first, meager step dealing with what we knew to be the Lord directing us. We simply decided we weren't going to ignore and we weren't going to side step. We were going to say yes to adoption.

We had to be relentless in this decision, and we knew it from the very beginning. We had no idea what was ahead, nor did we have any idea what steps one must take to adopt. We only knew that, physically speaking, this thing seemed impossible, but we could not deny God's direction. Danny and I both discussed all the challenges we would be facing in this pursuit. We then reminded each other of the one thing that mattered, which we knew in our Spirit we had going for us; the Lord. We had to set our faces like flint and be determined to be obedient before we made a single step. We had to because we could already see that there would soon be instances where we could possibly waiver in our obedience if we looked at our own capabilities and resources.

It took two or three months before we finally had the nerve to tell anyone else. Those few months were woven with much research and prayer. Both of us were constantly brought back to one place- Peru. It was very strange, really. Neither of us had ever been to Peru or South America at all, for that matter. Somehow, from the very beginning, it became clear to us that we were to adopt from Peru.

It was exhausting. All of the digging, and truly, all of the discouragement. It became increasingly apparent that Peru wasn't the easiest country from which to adopt. I soon found that there were only three agencies in the US who worked with Peru at all. I talked with one agency who told us that the Peru program probably wasn't for us due to the ages of our children. They explained that Peru rarely, if ever, allowed families to adopt whose biological children were as young as ours. Next, we were told by another agency that we did not qualify financially to adopt through their Peruvian adoption program. We didn't let this detour us. After all, if we didn't think we could take care of another child, we wouldn't be seeking to adopt. And even more so, God had clearly revealed to us our capability in Him. Finally, I called and spoke with the only other US agency that worked with Peru. It was a Christian agency equipped with people who seemed very down to earth and eager to see the fatherless placed into families.

We filled out an application with the agency, all the while being full of fear and what- ifs. I say "we," but in all honesty, this was more of a "me" struggle than anything. Danny seemed fearless and unwavering. " It will all work out," he reassured me. But it was hard to believe in the midst of all of the research that revealed more and more what a difficult and uncertain journey lay ahead. Both agencies who had discouraged us from Peruvian adoption were right. Our family's finances, based on one real income and the number of kids already in our household, were bordering on the poverty line set by US immigration. The line they were calling poverty, we could not see as such. It was an absurd thought. We were not wealthy by any means, but our only debt was our home, and we had what we considered to be ample income to take care of more children. It was difficult when I looked at the numbers and read about others who had spent years pursuing Peruvian adoption, to only be denied. I found many stories online of families who were still waiting to be matched with a child after four years. I could not even fathom waiting so long to bring a child home.

My thoughts seemed to turn continually to questions. What if we tell people God has led us to adopt and then end up being refused by the government or the agency because of our finances? What if we are refused because we live in a double wide trailer? What if we're refused because of the number of our children and their ages? What if we do everything the US government requires to adopt and then Peru ends up telling us no in the end?

After battling these fears for a while, I finally stepped out and announced our decision to adopt. Making this news public beyond our very inner circle seemed intimidating. I had already received responses like, "Yes. You might do that one day." And, "I guess if God told you to do that, then He can also make you grow two extra arms as well!!"

People meant well. They just saw our family growing as a burden and a struggle. It was just as evident to them as it was to us that we were already a busy family. It was difficult to explain to others that we knew God was leading us right then, at that very time to pursue adoption. It was a challenge to make them understand what we were merely trusting God to take care of in faith. It seemed outside of ourselves at the time. We were simply choosing to believe that God could handle all of those places where we felt incapable, and then I would secretly wrestle in "The Fear Battle" in privacy.

I blogged on July 7, 2010:

"We are adopting. We have completed our first of many applications and sent it to our agency. We are excited to fulfill God's plan for us. The last few months have been amazing. It has been truly miraculous to see God's hand leading us in this direction. We cannot deny it, or dodge it, and we don't want to!

I recently heard a very uplifting sermon. In the sermon the preacher talked about Psalm 139, and how 'All of the days ordained for me were written in His book, before one of them came to be.' We know God has a plan for us, but because of sin and because of us making choices on our own behalf, we often times don't fulfill what He has for us. The sermon was simply about how God never writes ordinary stories. There is

17

not a story in His Word that is ordinary. Every person that decides to submit his or her life, plans, and future into God's hand is never disappointed. He desires to use us mere humans to fulfill His work, and it is nothing short of awesome. I refuse to live my life and look back wondering what I should have done, but didn't do because I was too afraid, comfortable, or short-sighted to totally pour myself into the plans that He set in motion for me. It scares me to think my life is ticking by each day. I only list those fears and comforts because those are the flotation devices I usually find myself clinging to. It feels like this life is a raging storm, and when I look at my tiredness, time, money (lack of) dreams, etc... I often feel I will surely drown if I completely let go of it all and dump everything in me upside down. I cannot let my life be spent hanging on to these things I call security, even if my securities are merely excuses, when the only real security is Christ the solid Rock!"

Surprisingly, after the blog entry, we were mostly met with sincere love and support from everyone. Our closest friends and family members began to rally around us, encouraging in every imaginable way.

Our first application fee was $250, which was easily paid for. Soon after, we were officially accepted into the Peruvian adoption program with our agency. Excitement filled us as we stepped out into the unknown and saw God confirm our path with an unexpected "Yes!"

I wondered why I was so incredibly shocked by "Yes." No doubt we were pursuing God alone, and all because of His leading! Somehow, I had internally thought all of my what-ifs could trump God's plan in a willing vessel.

What a crazy thought! I knew in my core, and from scripture, that no man, government, or circumstance could stop God's plan from being fulfilled in a person fully surrendered and submitted. In fact, God gave us so many biblical examples of using the ordinary to do the extraordinary, that it seems rare to see any other equation at work! It's obvious that God finds pleasure in taking the most unlikely characters and using them for a task totally outside themselves. That's how God gets the glory. That's how we as humans are left in awe. When reflecting on the steadfast faith of so many biblical heroes, I wondered inside whether they were as scared as I.

Chapter 4

Confirmation

It was on another occasion early in our adoption process that God would meet me in the middle of my human frailty and fears. Soon after our first few applications were submitted, the work began. Along with the to-do list, there was a fee list. Danny and I were aware from the beginning that this adoption was expected to cost approximately $30,000. After getting over that initial shock, we placed that, too, in God's hands. Would God ask us to do something He could not provide for? I was asked many questions about why adoption was so expensive from people who were curious and skeptical that those fees were necessary or even ethical. As we looked at fees broken down into lists, it became obvious that there was not one man sitting behind a desk somewhere getting wealthy on adoptions (usually). The best way I could wrap my mind around it was imagining it as if the entire adoption process was a huge pie cut into about 200 pieces. Each piece was another legal requirement, and the very last piece was actually bringing our child home from Peru. Each piece of pie seemed to be some requirement taken care of by a different person, government, or organization. Every piece had its own fee. All of those pieces added up to a whole lot of moolah. Good thing our Father owned all of the cattle on a thousand hills!

I knew we would have to be immovable in our decision to forge through all of these endless requirements. I knew the only way that was even slightly possible was because of the immovable hand of God drawing us continually forward, urging us with his strength. Staring at that mountain of papers on our counter top looked like a few years worth of chores awaiting us. How could we ever fill out everything correctly? How could we complete every legal requirement, medical exam and test, social worker visit, and adoption education requirement? With each doubt, God would lead us on a little more. In the early morning hours when Danny and I would rise and cry out to God on our child in Peru's behalf, God gave us strength for each task. He would paint beautiful pictures in our day dreams of us embracing and loving, nurturing and raising the child that He had already placed in our hearts. These beautiful images of our beautiful child were the dreams that fueled us for the next task.

It was on one such morning where my great fears were greeted once again by God's measureless love. I had gone to bed the night before with a good bit on my mind. There were new fees staring us in the face. We had finally found a home study agency in Louisiana who could work with our agency that was out of state. Peru was a Hague Convention country. Essentially, that means that they were part of a convention of countries who had agreed to a list of legal requirements for any family to adopt from their country. The Hague countries were definitely more challenging to adopt from due to exhaustive requirements which were in place to protect innocent children all over the world and to help ensure that they'd be placed in good loving homes. We were required to use a Hague accredited home study agency, or one who could work hand-in-hand with our out-of-state agency. The latter of those two options seemed to be the only possible choice. Because of this, we were expected to pay approximately $2500 for the home study. Where was this money going to come from? While our bills were paid each month, leaving some excess, there was no way for us to produce the extra funds needed for the home study without setting money aside for several months. That could delay everything significantly and seemed to contradict the urgency we felt in our spirit over our Peruvian child's well being. We knew we were to schedule the home study right away, yet we did not have the money to pay for it.

One morning I awoke with the immediate reminder of our need. I sat down in my green recliner to pray just like most every morning. My heart was heavy, and my normal list of needs and thanksgivings couldn't break to the surface of the one burden that left everything smothered beneath. A sudden piercing brokenness and doubt swept over me.

"What were we doing?" I asked myself. "There would never be enough money to pay for the long list of fees knocking on our door! Even if we found some way to pay for this adoption with extra money here and there, it would take 10 years or better..."

My doubts rumbled on and on until finally I couldn't bear it anymore. Suddenly that heavily unbelieving pendulum made a switch. God showed me that I simply was not trusting Him. Plain and simple. I made an instantaneous decision to shift that burden to the only one who could carry it. It dawned on me, as if I'd never known it before, to tell my Abba Daddy what He had known all the time. I began to weep as I poured out my heart before the Lord. The tears fell in handfuls as I admitted to the Lord that my doubt and my fear were so much greater than my faith.

"God. You know we need this money. Oh, Father! We desire to do your will. This is all completely impossible for us. Every bit of it. Please show us what we are supposed to do here. Do you want us to take out a loan? Please show us what to do... We need to hear from you, Lord."

I did not go on with any of my normal prayers that morning. I simply prayed that one prayer, and then opened "Ol' Trusty." It was the devotion book I had read from nearly every morning and evening since I was a teenager. A church visitor had given it to me after a Sunday morning service when I was sixteen. She told me all about what a blessing it had been to her. I couldn't count the times God had used it in my life since. Daily Light was made of only scriptures taken from all over the Bible to form short devotions. I'm not sure there was any time before June 20, 2010, that God had used it so mightily in my life as He did the morning when I cried out to Him in desperation over our inability and the great needs we had in regard to our adoption.

I dried my tears and ended my prayer for direction regarding adoption funds, and I opened Daily Light and turned to that morning's devotion.

June 20

Take this child and nurse him for me, and I will give you your wages.

Go into the vineyard, and whatever is right I will give you. Whoever gives you a cup of water to drink in My name, because you belong to Christ, assuredly, I say to you, he will by no means lose his reward. The generous soul will be made rich, and he who waters will also be watered himself. God is not unjust to forget your work and labor of love...in that you have ministered to the saints, and do minister.

Each one will receive his own reward according to his own labor.

"Lord, when did we see You hungry and feed You, or thirsty and give You drink? When did we see You a stranger and take You in, or naked and clothe You? And the King will answer and say to them, "...Inasmuch as you did it to one of the least of these My brethren, you did it to Me." Come, you blessed of My Father, inherit the kingdom prepared for you from the foundation of the world.

(Exod . 2:9; Matt. 20:4; Mark 9:41; Prov. 11:25; Heb. 6:10; 1 Cor. 3:8; Matt. 25:37-38; 40, 34)**

I sat for a long time in silence, except for the sound of my own blubbering. God Himself had come to meet me in the pool of my own doubts and fears. I felt the praises and then courage rising up in me. God was holding this whole situation together. How dare I be afraid! He called, and He would supply! I sat and thanked Him for His goodness until I heard little feet coming to greet me with the sun. Danny soon arrived home from his morning time at the church, and I had the privilege of sharing the beautiful word God had spoken to me that morning. We shared some more tears together, and both suddenly felt strength and assurance where there had previously been such weariness and concern.

We decided after that to take out a small loan to pay for the home study. We battled whether or not we should take out the loan. But only a couple of weeks after that, all of the money had been paid back.

Danny and I had some friends drop by the house to say hello one evening. They stayed and visited for a bit, and as they were leaving, they handed Danny an envelope. After they were gone, we opened the envelope to find $1000. We were so blown away! We had never expressed our need to anyone, but God was providing. Only about two weeks later, another couple that are good friends of ours came by our house and gave us $500. It was as if the Body of Christ was gathering around us, cheering us toward that goal.

The generosity of our brothers and sisters in Christ spurned us forward and encouraged us. We immediately got to work planning fundraisers. There were a good many ideas that began to fill our heads. We began with a garage sale and shortly afterwards started planning another one. Friends and family began dropping bags and boxes by our home to contribute to the sale. TVs, exercise and music equipment, knick knacks and decor. We set up our sale at Danny's parents' home. They were both a success and brought in about $1500.

I started making "Aprons for Adoption." The frilly June Cleaver style aprons were a hit. I stayed up late at night sewing until my back ached and my vision blurred. I would sit and dream of holding our child. I knew with each stitch, each lacy hem, and each completed apron, we were one step closer to embracing our precious one. Those thoughts always gave me renewed strength. There were many a late night that all I could do was sit and weep at the thought that our child was waiting on a mommy and daddy to love and hold and comfort them. It would remind me to be diligent and work harder.

Danny got busy collecting scrap iron to sell for more adoption funding. Some of the iron required being cut into pieces. He spent his spare time with his cutting torch at work and hauling the iron to the local "Pack Man." Our church donated an old, broken down bus for scrap iron, and it added significantly to our funds.

After the word God had given me so directly regarding His provision, I began searching for a Hague accredited home study agency that would be able to come to our home for the required interviews and home visits. There was not one anywhere close by, so our adoption agency was able to work with a social worker and take care of that. I looked and looked for an advertised Christian home study agency, and found nothing. I was scared of this part of adoption! I could feel the what-ifs rising up again. How would some stranger see us, our parenting, our finances, and our beliefs? I had heard so many horror stories and couldn't seem to find many great ones to counteract the bad. I finally got some nerve and called one agency who had a social worker who worked in our area. They gave me her number, and I called her directly.

To my surprise, she turned out to be an incredibly friendly and understanding individual. We were sure she wouldn't be able to set up a meeting with us for at least a month. Another pleasant surprise came! She happened to also be a school social worker and was needed at school in only a couple of weeks. She told us it would be best for her if she could come do the first home visit on that upcoming weekend. We were elated!

I was also especially relieved because I had spent the entire day scrubbing our home top to bottom, even cleaning out our flower beds. I had not known the social worker would be coming in a matter of a few days when I had done the work. God knew though, and I guess He knew I would kill myself getting things spick and span, so He got me working in advance! It was solely for my own comfort, too. Our social worker was extremely down to earth and assured me over the phone that there would be no white glove tests on our home cleanliness.

Our social worker, Kim, arrived a week later. We had been praying fervently that everything would go smoothly with us, and with our children. Danny and I both had to be interviewed individually, and the children all had to be interviewed as well, at a subsequent home visit.

Grandmama and Grandaddy watched the boys for the first interviews. Kim put us both at ease, and our visits with her were actually enjoyable. We were interviewed about everything from our finances (down to the T), to our marriage, our pasts, and our parenting methods. We were asked why we wanted to adopt, and why we wanted more children. We were asked what we would do in certain situations and how we had prepared so far.

While I was being interviewed, Danny watched TV in our bedroom. When he told me what he'd been doing, I found it rather hilarious. While he was interviewed, I had my ear perched to the wall, listening to his every response! A good picture of the differences between us! While I had been banging my head against the wall as a reaction to some of his responses, he had been chilling out watching the Beverly Hillbillies during my interview! Oh, to be so relaxed!

Our children's interviews were just as hilarious. At least, looking back. Amaus scarcely let out a peep. Isaac answered in short monotone sentences. Josiah, on the other hand, answered the questions in the most humiliating and surprising way. It sounded like a sitcom script. Kim asked Josiah what he liked to do with his parents. He responded, "I like to play checkers, but they never have the time."

As I picked up my jaw off the floor, I wondered when Josiah had acquired this alleged love for checkers. I could remember him asking me once to play checkers, and I wasn't able to at the exact moment he had asked. It had never been mentioned again! I guess it had become his new favorite hobby overnight! We still get a good laugh about that experience! Thank God Kim knew kids and was familiar with how they often expound on some details, while leaving others out.

There was a whole lot more to completing a home study than simple home interviews. Our entire family had to undergo physicals and blood work. Several friends and family members had to write letters of recommendation for us. We turned in numerous financial sheets and tax refunds.

We weren't sure how long the home study would take to complete. We had plenty to keep us busy in the meantime. Adoption from a Hague convention country requires several different training sessions, including an online adoption class, tests and reading some encyclopedia-sized books and articles. That, along with filling out our US immigration paperwork (I-800A, petition to the US government to adopt a child from a Hague convention country), kept us occupied.

I continued to sew "Aprons for Adoption," and we planned another garage sale. We also had a barbecue chicken dinner plate sale that brought in about $1500. Several people came out of the woodwork and donated money towards the adoption. A sweet lady at church gave us $100. Another incredible lady gave us $50. My husband preached at a church, and they took up an offering for our adoption expenses bringing in about $500. We continued to be humbled and grateful. It was miraculous what was happening, and we knew it.

My sister planned a softball tournament. Several churches and friends were able to participate. It raised right over $1000. A friend and fellow worship leader from church hosted a Tupperware party that made a few hundred dollars as well. At every turn, and at every corner where a fee awaited us, the money was always waiting there to meet us just in the nick of time.

During that summer, shortly after we had stepped up to begin the process, Danny and I took a group of youth, along with our church youth pastors, to Six Flags for a weekend event. A few days before we were supposed to leave, I began to have pretty serious back pain. It felt like I had a severely pinched nerve, and it was a struggle to walk. I was torn because we had been pumping our oldest two sons up for the trip for more than a month. If I didn't go along, they probably couldn't either.

I ended up taking some pain relievers and gritting my teeth for the trip. It was extremely hot, July weather in Texas, but our group was beyond excited about getting to ride rides and enjoying the weekend concerts. I love to ride roller coasters, and anything that doesn't spin in circles, and I intended to ride rides and have a good time that weekend, regardless of having to walk like a robot. It probably wasn't the wisest choice I've ever made. But...you know! It would be my oldest son's first time riding roller coasters! I couldn't miss that!!

We walked into the park, and the very first ride everyone insisted jumping on was a huge spinning sombrero. Oy! No thank you, ma'm. I sat at a group of tables that were parallel to the "ahem, stomach churn" and waited on the boys.

A few minutes later, a tall slender lady wearing a sun visor approached me and asked if she could share my table. "Sure!" I responded, and we were quickly caught up in conversation.

The lady asked me how old my children were, and conversation quickly shifted to our family's recent decision to adopt from Peru. "Oh!" the lady exclaimed. "I grew up in Peru. My family were missionaries in Lima!" I sat amazed at the very obvious God appointment before me. I immediately was glad I had braved the trip with an aching back.

The lady continued to ask me about the process. "What made you choose Peru? Have you ever been to Peru?" I began to explain, as quickly as I could, the journey we had already been on. I told her about my dream, feeling incredibly open and comfortable with this complete stranger. She stood up as the kids began to exit the spinning sombrero and said something that has stuck with me since.

"Well, I guess you guys chose to adopt from Peru because that's just where the cries were coming from!"

She hit the nail on the head. Yes. That's where the cries were coming from, and we were doing all we knew we should to get to them as quickly as possible.

Chapter 5

Hard Realities

After researching the great need for adoptive parents in Peru, with over an estimated 500,000 orphans, I had wrongly assumed in the beginning that it would be easy to adopt from Peru. The more I researched, the more people I talked to, and the more I asked questions, the more a hard reality began to surface beneath the shroud of my expectations and hopes. It seemed many people in the adoption world were finding out that most of these Peruvian children were locked tightly away in the chains of politics and bureaucracy. It was a crying shame to me. I followed many new stories of families who visited Peru and saw the many homeless street kids, and they too, decided they could and would love to be able to adopt one of these precious children. Unfortunately, that was much easier said than done. As I was finding out, Peru was one of the most difficult countries to adopt from and had one of the longest waits.

When people gave me these hard truths, I truly would let them roll in one ear and out the other. While some people do well with expecting the worst possible outcomes and longest possible waits, in order that they may be pleasantly surprised with the opposite, I operate quite differently. I always expect the best possible thing to happen. It's a pretty strange philosophy coming from someone who never wins anything or never gets the outcome I typically expect. But I can't handle the "expect the worst" mentality. When things don't turn out the way I hope, I am temporarily disappointed. But I get over it quickly and then set a new, often "naively positive" (as some might say), goal all over again. When I read in our agency paperwork that Peruvian adoption took somewhere around 18-24 months, I laughed and expected us to be traveling to Peru in a year. I remember the conversation quite vividly. Danny and I were driving on the Natchez Trace and discussing when we thought we'd be heading to Peru. I read the timeline out to Danny from the huge packet of paperwork I had sitting on my lap. Peruvian adoption couldn't possibly take 2 years! What in the world? I assured myself that we would be bringing our child home in 12-14 months without a hitch.

It wasn't until we had spent much time in the Peruvian Adoption process that I faced the hard reality of what was typical for Peru. Our agency worked with the Peruvian Priority Adoptions list. This list was made up of children who are considered less likely to be placed in families in Peru. They are children who have special needs, sibling groups, and older children. We were finally told that it was very rare to see younger children on the list without severe special needs. Danny and I did not think our child would have special needs, to be honest. We also didn't expect our child to be older. This posed a problem when our home study had to be one that would be acceptable by Peru, and by the US government, but also written out to express what we wanted in a child. Actually, it was pointless to step forward any further with Peruvian adoption unless we were open to an older child or a child with special needs. It posed a conflict considering we knew God was telling us to step forward. Were our expectations for our child out of line?

I felt frail and afraid before God when I finally lay down my expectation of what I wanted in a child at His feet. It hurt. Danny and I began to pray daily that God would show us the age range we should seek approval for. Then, the number of children we should seek approval for. Finally, the hardest decisions seemed to lie in what degree of special needs we should seek approval.

We were told by various people who had walked the adoption path before us, and our agency, that it would be best for us to seek a broad approval, because changing our minds later down the road could mean further delays. We would have to come back and change things if we ended up deciding later to adopt a sibling group or a child with more severe special needs.

One afternoon, Danny and I kneeled beside our couch and prayed for God to give us clarity on the issue of what kind of approval we should be seeking. We strangely both opened our eyes to the realization that the child God had for us just might not be a baby. What if He had two children for us? We ended up deciding to seek approval to adopt up to two children, boy or girl, with or without mild to moderate special needs.

We both believed without a doubt that God had at least one little girl for us. Other than that, we had no real expectations anymore.

One day early on in our decision to adopt, I happened upon a website of an orphanage in Peru. I fell in love with three precious baby girls. I followed the blog and orphanage pictures avidly. When the pictures were finally updated on the site, I realized that the three little girls weren't actually babies anymore. They were four or five years old. One day, I decided to ask our agency about the little girls at the home. I was beyond surprised when our social worker from the adoption agency told me that they worked a good bit with that orphanage and that they had been able to facilitate several adoptions from there. That really excited me! My wheels were spinning! What if?

There was one little girl in particular whom I wanted to ask about. Her name was Camila.

I had loved the name Camila and had actually picked it out during two of my pregnancies until I found out we were expecting sons. I pondered how crazy it would be to end up adopting a child named Camila.

One day I asked our agency social worker about that particular child. She told me she would be more than happy to check for us. It was agony as I waited a week for a response.

When I finally called and checked, we found out Camila had been adopted. I was very disappointed. Waiting was so difficult for me. It was even more difficult while not having a particular child to set my heart on. I so wanted something tangible to focus my waiting on.

I followed the other two little girls from the home and inquired several times about them, only to find out months down the road that we would never be able to adopt either of them because they were not going to be placed on the Peruvian Priority Adoption list. I had fixed my hopes on something, and God had to allow my hopes to crumble for me to realize the only place I should be placing my hope and expectations was in Jesus and the word He had given us to adopt.

Chapter 6

A Place To Grow

It was now January of 2011. We were quickly approaching a year of the marked date when we knew the Lord had first burdened our hearts to adopt. Our home study had been completed several months before, and we had only recently been able to submit the form we had been working on for so long. The I800a was mailed to the United States Citizenship and Immigration Services, along with our home study, and various other proofs that we were prepared in all ways for international adoption. We were told to expect a 90 day wait for a response or approval of that application. During that time, we would receive a biometric fingerprint appointment. I did not want to hear that we would be waiting 90 days! I sat down in my recliner and prayed that our biometric appointment would arrive soon. I opened my purse calendar and circled the following Tuesday. "The appointment will be in the mail, on this day! I just know it," I declared out loud. That following Tuesday, when I went outside to check the mail, inside I found our biometric appointment. What a miracle!

We waited and waited to get a word from immigration. No word came. We did our best to focus on the large sum of money we were still needing to pay for the adoption. I was no longer sewing aprons because the all night sew-a-thons had started to take a toll on my ability to overcome severe grouchiness. My mother-in-law helped me plan a third garage sale, and we got busy preparing for it. We applied for a grant with Show Hope and the Lydia fund.

In all of this waiting, I could feel the Lord peeling away the layers of my insecurity and my fear. The longer I waited, the more my expectations would change. I dreamed of the amazing joy of having our child with us for Christmas. I dreamed of fixing a little girl's hair. I dreamed of camping trips and family get-togethers.

During all of the dreaming, we began to get an extra bedroom ready. It was very timely because Josiah and Isaac had been begging to be able to share a room anyway. We bunked their beds, and they were thrilled. I moved another bed into the spare room and left it pretty simple as we waited on some news.

While we waited on news from US Immigration, we were able to begin on our next stack of paperwork called the dossier. It was a huge conglomerate of information that would be sent to Peru for review and hopefully a stamp of approval from the country. It entailed all of our financial and physical information, our home study, and basically any other imaginable details about us. We also had to prepare a scrapbook with photos of ourselves, home, extended family, hobbies, and pets. The scrapbook would be given to our child in Peru after we were matched as a way to prepare them for our arrival.

Making the scrapbook made things feel very close. To imagine that these papers and photos covered in bright stickers and detailed captions, were going to be given to our child, and that they would be holding it soon, made it feel only a hop, skip, and jump away.

Unfortunately, there were, yet again, more requirements for the dossier. Peru required that our whole family be assessed by a psychologist who would have to write a report after an interview and psychological testing. This was terrifying to me! I looked through the phone book and called the only psychologist in our area. I set up an appointment for the following week.

Little did I know, this would be one of the most awkward experiences of my life. I approached the office, which was an old house converted into an office building. I didn't see anyone inside, and the front door left me feeling as if I should knock before entering. That's just what I did. There was no response, so I opened the door. It opened up into a narrow hallway that led to an open room at the end. I followed the hallway into what appeared to be a waiting area. The house smelled of cigarette smoke, and I felt more uncomfortable than ever in the empty building. I sat and looked at a magazine in complete silence for about five minutes, until I finally heard the back door open. A lady entered into the back door which was visible through a glassed in back porch. She locked that door behind her, and then entered the room I sat waiting in, locking that door behind her, as well. She walked by me and said, "I'm presuming you must be Mrs. Reed." I quickly stood up and extended my hand.

"Hi! I'm Calley Reed. Nice to meet you."

The psychologist looked down at my hand with a blank sort of stare and curled her hand toward her chest, making a snarling noise. I couldn't believe it! The lady didn't want to shake my hand! Her hand was still slightly extended, so I awkwardly grabbed the tips of her fingers, as if I didn't notice.

That first meeting made it clear to me that I should have asked for recommendations before just calling up the first psychologist I found. Our interview was extremely odd, in which at one point the doctor had me working long division problems after I mentioned that math had been my least favorite subject. I was so confused. Was she deciding if she thought I was smart enough to adopt? I was informed that I would have to bring our boys back and leave them with her in order that she might assess them. Everything in me said that I should not leave my children alone with this lady. She terrified me! I wouldn't expect less from them!

When I left the office, I called another adoptive mom and asked her if what I went through was normal. She assured me that it was not, and the majority of the psychologist's requests and expectations had nothing to do with what we needed for adoption. I cancelled our other appointments that very afternoon and began calling around in search of another psychologist.

Several people recommended a Christian psychologist in a town about two hours from where we lived. I set up an appointment with him and prayed all would go well. The psychologist was able to see our entire family in one day, which was great for us considering the drive.

A couple of weeks later our family headed out of town for our psychological evaluations. The entire vibe of the office was low key, and the staff was down to earth and friendly. We were immediately put at ease. I was the first to go back to be interviewed. The psychologist was a funny guy, and I felt the interview was going well.

During a psychological evaluation, you're asked various random questions. Who was Martin Luther King, Jr? What was the Renaissance? What are your hobbies? Why do you want to adopt? How did you meet your husband? The list goes on.

Shortly into the interview, he asked a question though, that had not been asked of me at all since we began the adoption process. To say that it caught me off guard would be an amazing understatement.

"Mrs. Reed, have you ever tried drugs?"

I could feel the blood rushing to my face. I had been asked so many questions throughout the adoption process.

"Have you ever been arrested for substance abuse?"

"Have you ever been addicted to drugs?"

But I did not recall ever being asked if I'd tried drugs. There was a wide range of drug use. A teenager could easily have used drugs but not necessarily be classified as addicted, and that also didn't necessarily mean they'd ever been arrested for using drugs. The other questions I could answer comfortably without feeling I was lying.

I knew the truth might hurt me. I had definitely tried drugs. During eighth to tenth grade, I found myself living in total rebellion. I had grown so sick of cliques and groups and attempting to fit into a mold that was so far from the weird personality I knew I was, I finally got a, forget-it-all mentality and found similar friends who shared this mindset. My attempts at belonging were short-lived. The Girbauds and Pepe jeans cheerleader stereotype of my day, that I'm certain my mom desired me to be, never appeased the creative and eccentric side of me that I felt I had to veil to belong. This masking of my true self wore me out. I finally decided to rebel on everything I had known as solid and truth and ran as fast as I could into darkness. I smoked marijuana on the weekends and eventually before school a few days a week. During that time I felt insecure, hopeless, and unable to really relate with anyone. I still desperately wanted to fit in, even though I vocalized the opposite so loudly. I now succumbed to morphing into a new person to belong to this new group of people who were running into darkness just as fast as I was. It wasn't until the end of my sophomore year, that I came running home to Jesus with a broken and repentant heart. I have never been the same since. Jesus had literally changed me from the inside out. There was no looking back or turning around after the revolution that had taken place in my heart.

I never could have expected, though, that my past would come back and haunt me. Here it undeniably was, looking me dead in the face. It felt like I had an enemy asking me to declare amongst a party of friends that I had some sort of long lost allegiance to them and their evil ways.

What if this interfered with our entire process? What if this one truth ruined everything? What was I going to do?

Before I had time to reason, before I really even thought of what it meant, "No," popped out of my mouth. I was flooded with immediate doubt and desperately wished I could stretch out my arms at the speed of sound to retrieve the deception I had just let tumble from my lips.

"No," was such a simple word. Yet it felt to be a heavy ball and chain now pulling me deep into a black sea.

I sat pitifully with my head hanging, as the rest of the questions all blurred into space, and as the minutes rolled by I became increasingly aware of what I'd done. I could feel myself getting extremely hot, and sweat began to form on my forehead. I had just lied. I really just lied. I had actually lied to this psychologist! My heart was full of conviction. I really was appalled at myself! I had taken matters into my own hands in fear that God couldn't handle His own plans, and now it was almost unbearable to sit through the rest of the interview. I searched for a window of opportunity to try and fix my thoughtless blurp. Another question maybe, along similar lines. It never came. There never was a convenient opportunity to correct my wrong as the questions rolled into my ears by the dozen. I, the pastor's wife, a child of the Most High, had just lied because I was afraid of the consequences of my past sins.

When I left the psychologist's office, I was taken to a small room to begin the written psychological tests. Danny soon joined me in the same room. When the door closed, I quickly confessed to him that I had just lied to the psychologist. I think he was shocked because he didn't say anything at first, and that's a rarity for him. Why wouldn't he be shocked with me? I was pretty shocked with myself.

"What should I do?" I asked Danny. I was still battling what would happen if I told the truth. I felt like a young child who had been caught sneaking cookies before supper. Good grief! Why did I have to do something so ridiculous?

"Well, all I know," Danny responded, "is that we cannot expect God to bless our adoption if we aren't honest. God always blesses honesty."

I can always count on Danny to put me in my place and urge me to do what others would assure me was no big deal to look over.

I knew what I needed to do. I left the small room and asked the secretary to please send the psychologist by the room where we were taking our tests when he was available. As I scribbled in the bubble grid of my test waiting on the doctor to reappear, I wondered what his response would be to this patient who had so willingly lied. And all this while expecting him to write a report on what a wonderful, upstanding person I was! Wow. I really had some nerve!

Finally, the doctor returned. He quietly stuck his head in the door and I muttered something about how I needed to talk to him. This definitely felt exactly like the time I had to go and confess to my dad that it had been me who had broken all of the glass Christmas ornaments in the driveway in my seven-year-old attempt to make glitter. Yep. It felt exactly the same.

So I opened my mouth at probably a mouse's volume and began to confess to the psychologist that I had not answered honestly on one question. I immediately began to tear up, and the tension in the room was high. Danny continued to take his test (or at least pretend to) and I went on to confess that I had, in fact, tried drugs.

I tried to judge his facial reaction to this crazy lady admitting to lying. His face seemed undeterred by my confession and not in the least bit taken aback. His response was simply, "Well, I intend to write up the report just as I'd planned to before. Now I also know you have a conscience." He shut the door without another thought and that was that. You could almost hear the sigh of relief coming from me. There is truly nothing like the peace that follows making wrong things right. Oh, the relief. Oh, the humility. I was beyond glad to have that behind me. The dossier work continued forward. We also had to include new health physicals, blood work, and tuberculosis skin tests from our entire family. New appointments were made, and we managed to rush through all of those procedures in record time. We couldn't mail this new stack of documents that made up the dossier to Peru until we had received immigration approval to adopt, which seemed to be taking an eternity.

Finally, after what felt to be an extremely long wait, one day I went to check the mail to find our I-800A approval waiting in the box. I couldn't have been more excited. Now our family could finally mail our dossier to Peru!

This I-800A approval also allowed us to be able to begin viewing the Peruvian Priority Adoption list of children who were waiting for homes! Our very child could be waiting on that list!

We immediately received the latest Peruvian Priority Adoption list. What excitement filled our expectant hearts as we opened and downloaded the document. What if our child or children were on that very list?

The list was divided into categories of children based on their age, if they had significant special needs, and if they were a part of a sibling group. The list provided very little information at all. The only way to really know more in-depth information was to request the child's entire file. Danny and I decided to request the files for four little girls we saw on the list. The agency was able to provide me with two of those files very quickly.

I'll never forget the rush of emotions as I opened those files, and the subsequent ones that came later. There was a hope like no other that somehow our very child would be waiting inside. Some of the files came with one or two simple, often blurry, photos of the children. Many times I wept uncontrollably to see the blank and depressed faces staring back at me across the computer screen. The faces haunted me and left me in wonder of how we would ever know for sure which child or children were ours.

I would weep at times because I was moved with compassion for all of these children who were waiting for homes. I would also weep when I suddenly knew deep in my heart that the child I was viewing was not to be mine.

It turned out that all of the previous waiting and disappointment could not compare with the pressure that came from having the responsibility of choosing one's child. I grew weary as month after month we saw the files of children who we hoped were to be ours, only to realize they were not to be.

When all of these precious children needed homes, how could we wait forever? We knew for certain God had directly spoken to us in various ways along the adoption path, and we continued to stand, though maybe on shaky feet, that He would speak once again when the time was right.

There was one file I had come back to several times. A precious two-year-old little girl named Rosa. Her file showed that it was suspected that she might have fetal alcohol syndrome. I knew very little about FAS, and began researching it avidly.

That Memorial weekend my mother rented a condo and invited the boys and I to come spend a few days with her at the beach. I was so weary in our adoption journey. It seemed as if we were never going to find our child. While at the beach, I was sent a precious photograph of sweet little Rosa. Her face seemed to show the features of FAS, although I couldn't be certain they weren't simply the features of her particular ethnicity. She was absolutely beautiful. I loved this little girl, though she was thousands of miles away. I called Danny, who was back at home. He too, saw her photograph...he knew almost immediately that this child was not to be our daughter.

Later that evening, after a long day of hunting for seashells and riding the boogie board with the boys, Danny called to confirm to me finally that he did not believe the child was ours. I was broken-hearted. Everything I read about FAS scared me, honestly. But I had questions about what God might call us as a family to do. What if God had called us to adopt a child with FAS? If He did, He would undoubtedly equip us. I did my best to step outside of my own expectations and clear my mind in consideration of the possibility, but I had doubts that she was ours, just as Danny had spoken.

Danny and I decided, even after our first doubts, to have her full file translated. We were sent about 8 pictures of Rosa, all so precious beyond imagination. We had a consultation over the phone with an International Adoption Clinic about her file. The doctor there was very helpful, but honest about what should be expected if we chose to adopt a child with FAS. It was very sobering.

Danny and I prayed continuously over Rosa and the possibility of her being our daughter. We wanted what God wanted for us above all. We wanted to be willing to do whatever God might call us to do. After much prayer and consideration, we came to accept the fact that our first doubts were God's leading. We knew God had a home in mind for this beautiful little girl, and we mourned that it was not to be ours...but also found rest in knowing His will. We believed He had a family picked out for this special little girl, and we prayed that family would be bringing little Rosa home soon.

Right after this experience, the Lord gave me an amazing scripture regarding His plans for us. Once again, I seemed to find myself afraid. Afraid of what condition our child might be in when we finally met them. Afraid that I would not know His plan, or it might be much harder than I was prepared for. As I prayed for Him to remove all of my fears surrounding our child, God directed me straight to Isaiah Chapter 65, verse 23.

They shall not bring forth their children for trouble. For they shall be the descendants of the blessed of the Lord, and their offspring with them.

This scripture was written to the children of Israel, but I knew that God had given it to me that day as I chose to swim in fear just a bit more. It became a rock when people approached me with horror stories about those they knew who had adopted and had terrible experiences. There were people who had a story to tell about something they'd seen on TV and how I should be prepared for something horrible because of it. It was a great opportunity from Satan for me to be tempted once again to be afraid of what might be ahead for us. Dwelling on this scripture from Isaiah helped because I knew the heart of the Father. The same One who loved to place the lonely in families (Psalm 68:6) also loved to bring about victory in the lives of anyone who would allow Him to. I thought a good deal about the fact that all throughout scripture, and all throughout time, God always has had victory in mind for His people! I refused to be afraid and believe the lies of the enemy about unavoidable turmoil and rebellion that would certainly be a part of my future, according to some people, if we adopted a child!

We were being obedient to the Most High God, and we weren't going to accept that there was anything but victory in store for our child and our futures. That wouldn't always mean an easy road that didn't have it's share of trials. But I knew in my spirit, and through it all, God would certainly work out a miraculous victory that He alone could bring about. Our child would be stepping under the same banner that our current children had refuge under. The banner of a righteous heritage, and one that we would train all of our children in, Period. There couldn't be any place for fear about the future of my family or my children if I wanted to trust God.

Since we were not approved to adopt in Peru yet, we could not technically request a particular child from the list of waiting children. After all, we were still compiling the long list of documents that made up our Dossier to send to Peru. Thankfully, the list was finally nearing its end. We were still able to view the list in preparation for being able to request a child, but we were reminded over and over again that the possibility was always there that any particular child that we fell in love with could be adopted by the time we were actually able to request them. Every time I was reminded of this, it was a new opportunity to combat fear, doubt, and unbelief. The fleshly thought hung over my head: What if we found our child, and someone else adopted them before we received our approval to adopt?

God began to use these types of circumstance to spurn reflection on my true level of faith. Was He in fact my Lord, and did I truly believe He had the power to orchestrate, protect, and lead every aspect of this story? Or were these only religious words I was used to saying, but when the rubber met the road, my heart was far, far from believing them?

One particular day, anxiety began to build up in me as I dwelled on our child and his or her conditions and whether he or she would be adopted before we were able to make a request. I recognized that, once again, fear and faith were colliding within myself. The Lord did what I was beginning to see as a pattern in my struggles. He led me straight to a place in His Word to stand. It was always just what I needed; The sword I could use to do one-on-one combat with every doubt that would arise against the word I knew we already had from Jesus.

On that particular day, as I felt extremely weak in my defenses, I opened directly to the Psalms, chapter 16, verses 5-11, and began reading.

O Lord, You are the portion of my inheritance and my cup;
You maintain my lot. The lines have fallen for me in pleasant places; Surely I have a good inheritance.
I will bless the Lord who has given me counsel;
My heart also instructs me in the night seasons.
I have set the Lord always before me,
Because He is at my right hand I shall not be moved.
Therefore my heart is glad, and my glory rejoices;
My flesh also will rest in hope.
For you will not leave my soul in Sheol,
Nor will You allow Your Holy One to see corruption.
You will show me the path of life;
In Your presence is fullness of joy;
At Your right hand are pleasures forevermore.

Yes, exactly what I needed. God alone maintained our lot! He had a child or children for us, and He already knew who they were! He was preparing them for us and us for them. It would be perfect because it would be His perfect plan. The lines had fallen for us in pleasant places. We could not plan out or scheme up any greater plan than the one that the Lord alone could work on our behalf. And because we trusted in Him, we would not be shaken. His Word said it. I believed it.

I had to stand on these sorts of promises with more determination and more solidity than I ever had been required in my life. The waiting grew difficult. The only way I maintained sanity was by going back and remembering what God's Word had made plain.

Knowing we were marching forward with God's blessing helped us counteract other facts that we learned in the wait. Through the training we were required to undergo to adopt from a Hague convention country, we learned that there could be severe repercussions for children who had spent any amount of time in an orphanage or institution. Sometimes the affects of neglect, abuse, and abandonment left deep, deep scars that often come out through various behaviors. We were told that no medical information could be absolutely banked on, and just as with having a biological child, one should expect that there could be more health issues, delays, and issues discovered after arriving home with an adopted child, and even throughout life.

It was obvious that the longer a child had to stay in this institutional setting without a mommy or daddy to show them love and affection, responding to their needs and desire for attention, the harder it seemed to be to help them understand that they were, in fact, finally loved and wanted after being placed into a forever family.

It was funny to talk to people about international adoption. I think most of the mass populous viewed it the way we once had. And why wouldn't they? Most people thought that we should be able to go pick up a perfectly healthy, unscathed child that would kiss us on the cheek, embrace us, and never look back or question his or her early years of tragedy nor show any remembrance or after effects of it. This is a close to impossible feat. We were learning that even children who are adopted at birth will have questions and have to deal with the loss of knowing they were put up for adoption by their biological parents. Children who are older and remember their experiences in an institution will not usually understand and acknowledge that someone has come to give them a better life. There are real issues we knew we would have to face, but we also knew that the same God who had adopted us into His family and healed us of our past issues could do the same for anyone who trusted Him. Knowing that, we continued to rest in the loving hands of the One who had started our steps on the road to adopt.

Chapter 7

Unconventional Mama

Being a birth doula, I naturally found crazy similarities between the adoption process and the actual process of carrying a child and giving birth. One very prevalent similarity, to me, was found with the authorities who often direct and dictate both processes. I am an advocate for mothers and the right they have to birth in any way or setting they choose, and I am a servant to mothers in the birth process, striving to cheer them on to their goals. So often in certain birth settings, women are controlled by a doctor and a hospital staff's fear of litigation, and the amazing act of giving birth is treated as a one-size-fits-all process. Mothers are often pushed through a "birth factory" by being hooked up to machines and sent out of the way to make room for the next paying customer. Often times, the workers in this type setting aren't very compassionate or helpful to accommodate moms who want a less "factory" like experience. This is partially because they see so many mothers come through every day, so many babies wheeled off to the nursery, that the sheer miraculousness of what has just come to pass has been reduced to a mere business transaction. There is very little wonder and awe of the beautiful process of giving birth through that misguided mindset. When birth is treated in this regard, it teaches a society that birth is dependent solely on a medical team and a hospital staff. It has nothing at all to do with a wise Creator who didn't leave anything out when He formed mankind.

I was beginning to come to the conclusion that it was much the same with the adoption process. While agencies were surely not completely void of understanding and compassion, many phases were treated as stagnantly unofficial and routine. This became clear through some of the responses and viewpoints we received. When we shared our amazement of being aware of God's hand, we were often met with responses that attempted to knock us down a notch. It became increasingly evident that very few people, in general, actually trusted and believed that God still spoke directly to man, or even directed man's steps. That hurt. I could not deny and never would attempt to disregard the blatant ways the Lord had spoken and led our lives. Sometimes when I shared these miracles with certain individuals who had become familiar with adoption and the way it worked, I was treated as if I was lying, or dreamed up these undeniable circumstances. This even happened at times in Christian circles. To deny that my Jesus still spoke to His children was to deny my Lord Himself. To deny that my Jesus had already worked wondrous things to lead our family would be a slap in the face of my God. A slap of ungratefulness and a stance of humanistic selfishness that I could never take and claim as a follower of Jesus Christ. My God is alive and the same yesterday, today and forever. I would certainly never deny His ability to speak and lead and direct and work any wonder He saw fit, at any point in time or creation that He dared because He Is God. I'm just the man.

I have always been a question asker. When I began to ask questions regarding Americanized birthing practices, I found that so many things were done based on what had been done for years. Many times even nurses and physicians, without question, would assume that common modern practices were best for moms and babes alike. People aren't often happy with question askers because it knocks them off their routine, and if they like control, it makes them feel that their power is being threatened. It doesn't matter if it is a perfectly legitimate question- many people in places of authority feel that things operate much smoother without someone who digs behind the scenes to get to the bottom of stated routine policies to see what is really truth and what is really best.

When I asked questions throughout the adoption process, I found this to be true at times. I could be told

49

something wasn't possible, and then later, after much research, discover that it was possible, just not convenient for an agency. I could be told something couldn't be done any faster, to later find out that it actually could, but it might require a little extra work on someone's part.

We came to places that we had to speak up and advocate for what we felt would be best for our child, even if someone else didn't. We also came to places where we knew we might not be getting all of the facts, but the Lord would still urge us to "Hold our peace because He was fighting for us." (Exodus 14:14)

We became guardians over the words that God was giving us, being as careful as possible not to "Cast our pearls before swine." It seemed that we needed an army to stand and believe with us in faith, and not discouragers who would unknowingly place doubt in our hearts. We were determined to not allow those who weren't willing to rejoice with us to detour us. When people who were familiar with the adoption process were not amazed by the miracles we saw, our extended family, church family, and other adoptive families we had gotten to know certainly were.

Our church and extended family became like a strong net holding us up with encouragement when we felt weary. I became a member of a Christian Peruvian adoption group, and they encouraged us to stand on God's Word at every turn. This support was always there when we needed it most; no doubt, divinely placed by Jesus Himself.

There were several key people in this Peruvian adoption group who became dear friends to me. I was able to follow several of their stories to Peru and home. I was learning what to expect and how to overcome hard situations through these incredible families who had surrendered their all to the Lord's call to adopt.

Chapter 8

The Cord of God's Word

One beautifully joyful day at the end of February in 2012, we finally had everything we needed to be able to submit our dossier to Peru. Our agency told us not to expect to hear anything back for about two months. If we heard back from Peru, it would be to make corrections to our dossier. It was common for Peru to want clarification on various subjects in the dossier. It was also common for Peru to request other proof of a family's ability to take care of an adopted child.

We waited and waited and waited. I often wondered how long it could possibly take to review those papers? It sure felt like we must be at the very bottom of an extremely long list.

But just as we'd been warned, after two full months, we finally received a response from Peru. Unfortunately, it was not the response we had been hoping and praying for. Peru wanted further clarification on our finances and also more proof through an interview with a social worker that we could take care of another child along with our three sons, especially Amaus, who was still only two years old.

It was a hard blow after such a long wait, but a blow we should have expected since it was so common amongst all of the other Peruvian adoptive families we had gotten to know. But it seemed we had already gone to such extreme length to prove that we were capable of taking care of another child! Why more? I had a really good sob, took some deep breaths, and tried to muster up the strength needed to begin tackling the new requests.

New financial sheets were filled out, new company letters, new tax refund slips, new proofs of income were gathered, and new interviews were set up. Before too long, our requested stack of documents were tackled and sent to Peru to await review. We asked how long this second review should take, but no one really knew for sure. It seemed to vary with each family. Once again, we prayed and held on in eagerness for any bit or morsel of news from Peru.

Hanging in uncertainty, waiting without any tiny speck of something tangible was a difficult place for me to abide. There was no prospective child in our sites. We hoped and hoped every month that the list would reveal a new child that seemed to be within the bounds of our approval, but that child never showed up in the email we received once a month. My mind often drifted off to an imaginary vision of my child, always a little girl. She was around two or three, and she had tiny little pig tails on the sides of her head. She had beautiful caramel skin and the biggest, sweetest black eyes that I had ever seen. I pictured the precious little girl with a little apron, helping me in the kitchen, and having tea parties with her dollies. I imagined her climbing into my lap while I told her the stories of how God brought us all the way to Peru to bring her home. In my visions of my little girl, I told her what a special treasure she was, how we had loved her from the very first day God had placed her on our hearts. I would hold and rock her as I sang lullabies to her.

Those day dreams were the only thing I had to picture when I thought of our child. All that I could do was hang up the little picture in my mind and hope it stuck for later, and then I would move forward with the next task.

The interrupted hopes and constantly detouring paths that led to wherever our child was waiting for us was disheartening, to say the least. To dream of a child that I seemed to never know when I would finally hold; to want so desperately to have some future date to set my eyes on, only to be told that it would still be a long time yet...it was really ripping me apart. One day I decided that all that I could do was put my heart on the shelf, with all of its desire to protect and nurture, with all of its sentimentalism and emotional strings. It had to be packed away in a hard wooden box. It had to be packed away and stored up for a day when I could freely let it feel again without being disappointed. I didn't know how else to deal with knowing that we could still have a very long wait ahead of us. It just didn't seem right! Why, when all we wanted was to love and embrace the child that we knew Jesus had burdened us for? And why did Danny and I both still feel such an urgency inside that our child needed us, when we could no more speed up this process than we could change the seasons. So, I would pray for God to move, and then I would have to emotionally detach myself from all thoughts surrounding the process. It was too draining for me to know that my child was waiting on mommy and daddy to come and too stressful to count each second passing that he or she was having to wait longer. I was powerless to do anything about it, physically, so I would pray for the One who could do everything about it, to move on our behalf. Then I would withdraw my mind to a place of living day by day, where I had to simply pretend we really were not waiting to adopt.

One summer day, at the beginning of the week, I awoke with new courage and new enthusiasm. It was like a breath of fresh air that I'd needed for so long. I felt heavily impressed to go through God's Word and write on large note cards every scripture I could find pertaining to believing God above any circumstance. I dug into the Word and plastered scriptures from one end of our home to the other.

"Faithful is He who calls you, who also will do it*,'" hung on my bathroom mirror. "That your faith should not be in the wisdom of man, but the power of God*," now hung above the kitchen sink.

"Blessed is she who believed, for there will be a fulfillment of what was spoken her by the Lord*," was put by the coat rack. "As for God, His way is perfect. The Word of Jehovah is tried; He is a shield to all who take refuge in Him," was taped to my dresser vanity*.

53

I meditated on these scriptures all week. They were the only nourishment that could appease the weariness of waiting and the sadness of not yet finding our child. One scripture that I wrote on a note card was helping me to assess my thoughts and to realize their true root as being unbelief. "God is not a man that He should lie, nor the Son of Man that He should repent. Has He not said, and will He not do? Or has He spoken and will He not make it good?"

Did I really believe the great big God, Creator of the universe, and my King was working this out? Did I really believe?

(*1 Thessalonians 5:24, 1 Corinthians 2:5, Luke 1:45, Psalm 18:30, Numbers 23:19)

Chapter 9

God is Not Surprised

On Wednesday night, after I finished teaching the adult Bible study, I went in the church library to see if there was any book that I might pick up and read. Release the Power of Prayer, by George Mueller caught my eye right away.

Josiah and I had read George Mueller's life story as part of our home school curriculum the previous year. The biography impacted both of us greatly. Mueller lived a surrendered life and rescued thousands of orphans, always believing God to provide completely, and while never asking one person for money. He would pray, and God would send. There was always provision for the orphans, and God always made a way as this man prayed and believed against all physical odds. This story had such a strong impact on Josiah; in fact, that at the end of the book, he realized that he needed to be born again. We knelt in our living room floor and Josiah cried out to Jesus to be saved. It was one of my most precious moments as a mom.

I knew that I needed to learn more about prayer, and I was excited to begin this book about it, written by a man who lived a life of sincere faith and miraculous provision by God.

After church, I curled into bed that night and began to doze off. But I was soon awakened by the familiar sound of my phone "dinging" letting me know that I had received an email. I reached over and clicked the email icon. It was our social worker at our agency! What was going on?

I quickly read the email that began with, "Congrats! Today you received approval by Peru to adopt!" My heart seemed to skip a bit at the long awaited news. I woke Danny and told him as I rushed through the email to see what else it said. The email continued:

"However, the approval given by Peru was for one child, and the child must be at least one year younger than your youngest child."

I stopped hard, practically dropping my phone, and couldn't read or speak. It was all sinking in. This was not the news we had hoped for.

One child! At least one year younger than our youngest child!! How could this be? Our youngest child was only two years old. There had been only two to three children who had come through on the Priority Adoption List within that age range in somewhere around eight months! The only ones I knew of were severely sick and were not expected to live long. They had not even been on the list the last few months! What did this mean? If children of this age never came through on the only list we were eligible from which to adopt, how could we adopt at all?

I fell to pieces all at once. Danny didn't know what to say when I told him the news. I lay in bed and sobbed and sobbed until my pillow was soaked. Now our child seemed further away than ever before. It felt like they were lost in some distant dream, never to find their way to us through all of the junk that seemed to be constantly swimming in between our best efforts and good intentions to simply wrap them up in our arms and never let them go.

The next morning I awoke to the realization of the news I had received the night before. My thoughts were fuzzy.

Had we missed God? I cried all throughout the day and secretly wondered if somewhere we had gotten off step. But how and where? We had done only what we believed we were supposed to do throughout the months of waiting and praying.

What else could we have done? Had we gone wrong?

When I shared with others who were familiar with the Peruvian adoption process about the approval we had been given, no one knew quite what to say. It just didn't look good for us, and those people knew it. We all were sobered by the knowledge that kids that age were not found on this list very often, if at all, and that we could have an extremely long wait ahead of us.

I didn't feel I could wait any longer. In fact, if God himself had not spoken to us and directed us to adopt...I would have quit right then and there. Nothing in me desired to keep going forward with all of the stress and all of the struggling. Enough was enough, and I couldn't take the roller coaster anymore. I felt I was dangling by a cord, and it was only the cord of the Word the Lord had clearly given me. I could only grasp it with one hand, but knew I couldn't let go. Letting go would mean disobedience, and I knew that wasn't the answer, either.

Our agency talked to our representative in Peru, and she suggested that perhaps Peru was implying that they would prefer for us to wait until our children were older to adopt. That seemed to be their primary concern and the reasoning behind the approval they had given to our family. Could we take care of another child, possibly with special needs, and our current children (especially with already having a two year old)?

Our agency asked us if we might like to take a break from viewing the priority adoption list; that maybe we should step back, reassess, and pray to clear our minds a bit.

We quickly responded with a big, fat "No thank you!" We knew that we had begun the adoption process right when the Lord had prompted us to. In our best efforts, we could not understand or explain our very negative approval given from Peru, but we also knew we could not sit back and rest. Our child was out there waiting somewhere, whoever and wherever they were, and there had to be a reason for the sense of urgency we had held for them from the very beginning.

It was a day or two later as I vacuumed the house that the Lord overwhelmed me with the ridiculousness of my doubts. Some words rang in my heart that another Peruvian adoptive mom had spoken to me. "None of this has taken God by surprise!"

How dare I doubt my Lord! He knew that this was coming all the time, and nothing had changed in regard to His plans and His authority over the situation.

I stood in a daze looking out my kitchen window later that day, thinking again about our approvals. As I stood there, my mind thousands of miles away from home, pondering where we were, my eyes finally came to focus on the note card I had hung earlier in the week. "Faithful is He who calls, who also will do it. 1 Thessalonians 5:24."

My eyes welled up with tears and brimmed over, streaming down my face. The same God who was faithful to call us would also be faithful to bring it to pass.

Wow. Just wow. God had known what I'd be facing and had led me to post all of the scriptures I'd need all throughout the house a few days before one of our hardest tests of faith, yet. He had called, He would do. Plain and simple. I walked all throughout our home, retracing my steps and reading each card carefully. They were all scriptures that spoke directly to my need to simply believe this was in God's hands.

Another friend sent me a message of encouragement with the scripture,

"As for God, His way is perfect. The Word of Jehovah is tried. He is a shield to all who take refuge in Him." (Psalm 18:30) This was also one of the ones God had given me earlier in the week. It had a complete new meaning for me now.

This way, this path, that God was paving for our family, was perfect. My greatest plans and schemes couldn't even compare with the wonderful story God was choosing to write. How could it? My thoughts were not His thoughts, and my ways were not His ways. Since according to His Word, God could also do more than I could think or imagine, then I didn't need to understand how He was going to work this deliverance. I just needed to believe that He would. He just would because He was Lord of all, and He said He would. End of story.

I raised my hands in praise that day at my kitchen sink. I worshiped Him and cried tears of joy, knowing our family and our child were resting in God's hands...the unshakable hands that fashioned the earth and that formed me in my mother's womb.

I now grasped tightly to the cord of God's Word. I made a deliberate choice to dwell on what He had to say and not what man had to say about the situation. Every time the doubts would rise up (which was very, very frequently), I'd find another one of my scripture cards and I would declare the words out loud.

A shift began to take place inside me. I completely surrendered the wait to the Lord. No matter how long, no matter how hard, I decided to stand on God's Word, which would undoubtedly come to pass. I suddenly realized Jesus was trying to teach me so much right in that difficult moment.

He overwhelmed me with the realization that I could walk through the wait with victory, receiving all that He had for me during that time, or I could walk through it with a heavy, negative, and unthankful heart. The choice was up to me. But if I was to choose misery, it was not God's fault! He had made a way for me to be joyful in all things, and if I didn't have joy, I couldn't blame that on anyone but myself.

The truth was, in my heart, I sincerely wanted what God wanted for me. I recognized that this experience was one that God was using to form me. Would I allow His gentle hands to form me, or would I fight Him for everything I was worth, staying exhausted and defeated the entire time? All at once, I wanted to learn what it was He was trying to teach me. What a shame it would be to walk through this wait never having grown and never having absorbed exactly what it was Jesus was trying to mature in me.

My prayer life began to change just like my heart was changing. I leaned on Jesus and began to trust that He knew best. I dove right into reading Release the Power of Prayer, the George Mueller book I had picked up that eventful Wednesday before we had received the notice of our approval from Peru.

The book rocked my world, to say the least. It is George Mueller's own account of instance after instance when God would call him to circumstances completely outside of his capabilities. The reports would be terrible and unfavorable. All of the resources he knew of would be exhausted. He would pray and watch the Lord work the miracles. There was not a single time that God did not provide for Mueller, the orphans under his care, and his family.

During that time, God brought me to a scripture .

Rise during the night and cry out. Pour out your heart like water before the Lord. Lift up your hands to him in prayer, pleading for your children, for in every street they are faint with hunger. Lamentations 2:19

The Lord wrote it on my heart. I had been praying since day one for our child, but suddenly God put a burning in my heart to pour out my heart like water before Him on behalf of our child. This was just what I was reading about in George Mueller's life simultaneously. Undoubtedly, God was teaching me how to pray for our child while standing in faith.

Another passage from God's Word that seemed to show up everywhere I looked was:

One day Jesus told his disciples a story to show that they should always pray and never give up. *"There was a judge in a certain city,"* he said, *"who, neither feared God nor cared about people. A widow of that city came to him repeatedly, saying, 'Give me justice in this dispute with my enemy.' The judge ignored her for a while, but finally he said to himself, 'I don't fear God or care about people, but this woman is driving me crazy. I'm going to see that she gets justice, because she is wearing me out with her constant requests!'" Luke 18:1-8.*

Then the Lord said, "Learn a lesson from this unjust judge. Even he rendered a just decision in the end. So don't you think God will surely give justice to his chosen people who cry out to him day and night? Will he keep putting them off? I tell you, he will grant justice to them quickly! But when the Son of Man returns, how many will he find on the earth who have faith?" It showed up again in the book I was reading as referenced by Mueller. I dwelled and dwelled on these words...

"And will God not avenge His own elect who cry out to Him day and night, though He bears long with them...I tell you He will avenge them, and speedily."

These scriptures struck me. There must be something to people getting so serious about a cause that they are willing to cry out in the night hour. A stance of desperation, and an outward willingness to inconvenience one self to pray on behalf of a serious need. Sometimes that desperation might be causing a lack of sleep anyway. But nonetheless, it's apparent that when God's people get so desperate that they pray day and night, constantly coming before Him for the sake of a desperate situation, things change and things move. There is truly something remarkable that takes place in the midst of this kind of brokenness.

Danny and I discussed this in depth and came to a decision. It was time for our prayers to get desperate. Even more desperate than they had been. It was time to place this request for our child, and his or her well being, at the forefront of our everything. This first stance of desperation came in the form of setting our alarm for three AM every morning. We sat up in bed and poured our hearts out like water before the Lord on behalf of our child.

Lord God, You alone know where our child is waiting. Please move governments, please move circumstances, and please move time to bring them home. We ask you, dear God, to do this thing that You alone can do! We are desperate for our child to be safe and in our arms. You placed this seed within our hearts, and God, we ask you to bring it to fruition, despite every negative report and every negative approval!

I inwardly struggled with the words I heard from everyone that said, "God's timing is best. It will come to pass when it should." God made it plain in scripture that He cared about the cause of the fatherless. If there was no need, we wouldn't be paying thousands of dollars and traveling thousands of miles away to go bring a child home! So obviously God preferred to 'set the lonely in families' as He claimed He did in Psalms 68:6. I reasoned in my heart, that no doubt it would be better off for the child to be home sooner rather than later. I wondered how much the Lord allowed to rest in our prayers and in our faith. It seemed to me, and I was finding as I studied God's Word in that time of seeking His heart, that from Moses to King Hezekiah, to the widow in Jesus' parable that cried out day and night...when people get desperate for the sake of others, or even themselves, and pour themselves out in that brokenness before the Lord, both heaven and earth are moved.

Enough was enough. Our child needed us, and we were desperate. We did not know our child. We did not know his or her condition. We did not know if they were being cared for or shown affection. We simply knew it was time to rumble schedules and priorities and everything in between to cry out to the Lord for his or her behalf.

I set my face like flint to scarcely let an hour pass without raising my hands to the One who would hear and answer. I fell on my living room floor about three times a day, on my face and prayed,

"Oh Lord, please move! Lord bring our child home to us! Dear God, surround our dear one with your everlasting arms. Please fight on behalf of our child, please bring our little one home."

Everywhere we went, we found out people were praying for us and our child. I would be at the grocery store and an acquaintance would tell us about how they had been praying every day for our family. One day I was stopped in Wal-Mart by a lady who said she made it her priority to pray for us and our waiting child every single day. I was dumb founded and humbled by this lady offering up her time to pray on our behalf.

I think I really began to learn what the Body of Christ was all about and what it meant to weep, rejoice, and pray for one another. Our family had never felt so loved and held up as we did when our community rallied around us to bless us in bringing our daughter home. It was an amazing thing to be a part of.

Our church family and various children at our church took on the role of praying fervently for our child. In the children's Sunday school class I taught, the kids testified of praying for our child each night before they went to bed. When requests were called out in a church meeting, our child was usually named by one of the kids.

Our prayers began to shift a little as well. We became more and more certain, by God's Spirit, that we would be getting a daughter.

Our sons prayed at every meal and at bedtime each day, "God please protect our little sister. Please God, bring her home as quickly as possible." Josiah usually added, "Please, dear Lord, please, please, please, please...bring our sister home soon. Please." I wish I could have counted all of the 'pleases' that went into his daily prayers.

Every time a new Peruvian Priority Adoptions List came in, I would practically lose my breath as I opened the attachment and scrolled through the list. Now I could scroll through it in no time, because I could search by age. It really narrowed the over four hundred names on the list down because there were scarcely few, if any at all, within the age range approval we had been given.

Chapter 10

When to Wait
When to Move

T ime moved forward, and for several months we stood in faith that God was doing something we could not see, despite the physical lack of movement that seemed absent as we waited and prayed.

One day, just like every month, I received a new list of waiting children. I went through the same routine of opening the list in a breathless hurry and scrolling through, when I came to a name on the list that caught my eye.

Camila. I could not recall a Camila on the list since we began viewing it. I read the small amount of information beside her name over and over again. "Responds to affection. Explores her environment."

Camila. What if the Lord had had a Camila for us all the time? This little Camila's age was listed out to the side. According to the list, she would be three years old, only two months after our youngest son, which was quickly approaching.

I sighed... knowing that meant she was too close to our youngest son's age, according to the approval Peru had given us. I thought on it some more, and I finally decided to call the agency and inquire about the little girl anyway.

Our agency was unsure about how Peru would respond to us requesting a child outside of the age approval they had given. In the end, we were discouraged from stepping forward any further. Peru might possibly take it that we had totally disregarded their advice to our family, and we did not want or need to come across that way to the authorities over our adoption process.

The next month passed, and my thoughts occasionally turned to the name on that list. Camila. I finally asked Danny about her again. We discussed it in depth and prayed about it. We both came to the same conclusion. What did we have to lose in requesting her information?

I called the agency back and expressed our viewpoint. What did we have to lose in requesting her information or even potentially requesting this little girl? Even the agency admitted that it would not affect our ability to adopt from Peru, even if they said no to a particular child. So we stepped out and requested her file. It would be translated and sent on to us.

It seemed like forever as we waited on the file to arrive. What would it say? What was this little girl's background, and how did she come to be an orphan? Would this all turn out to be a big waste of time and another rabbit chase in the end?

Finally, on a Wednesday night, several weeks down the road, the information about Camila came in the form of an email, as it typically did. I read through it, reread through it, and reread through it. The precious Peruvian little girl was significantly developmentally delayed. She was on seizure medication, although no information was given about what kind of seizures she was having, or how frequent they were (or actually, not even that they had ever occurred).

There was really little to no family medical history for Camila. She was taken off the streets at eight months of age, and there were really no known circumstances about her mother's pregnancy or birth. I wondered how they were certain of her date of birth without any of that information. Camila was also very small for her age, quickly approaching three years of age and still the size of a twelve to eighteen month old.

Danny also reviewed the file. We both had very obvious concerns but began to pray.

It was several weeks later before church one evening when I received an email that contained two photos of Camila. I had been waiting ever so anxiously to finally put a face with the few bits of information we had on her. I was so scared and eager, both at once, as I waited on the attachments to load. When the photos finally loaded and opened, I couldn't believe my eyes. Before me was one of the most beautiful little girls I had ever laid eyes on. She was dressed in a yellow and flowery outfit. She had a healthy round face and the largest and prettiest black eyes, so full of wonder. Camila had a huge smile and the photo was snapped of her in mid clap, both of her hands together. As her eyes seemed to look right at me across our laptop, she seemed to be so close, rather than across rivers and jungles and country borders. Her eyes were so attentive and bright, so alert. I was so overwhelmed by her that I just began weeping uncontrollably, and then began jumping up and down. It seemed crazy to me at the time, but for whatever reason, I was beyond thankful for this precious little girl, and I simply couldn't stop raising my hands in gratitude to the Lord for her. I called Danny and told him through tears that he had to open my email account and see what was inside. It was beyond amazing to see Camila before us, and our hopes began to rise.

From what we had learned in our Hague adoption training, and through other adoptive parents, many of the issues found in Camila's file could be from neglect. In fact, children will often be very behind in development, both mentally and physically, when there isn't someone there to continually love, play with, and nurture them. When a baby is not responded to when crying, he or she will eventually learn, through continuous neglect, that no one will respond. Sometimes that child may stop crying altogether.

Another result of neglect can be physically stunted growth due to not only inadequate nutrition but also little interaction and attention.

Obviously, there could be deeper roots to these delays and Camila's small size. These issues could range anywhere from parental drug abuse to sickness or brain injury. We might never the cause.

We had no idea what was behind the things in her file, but we began to simply set our face on the Lord, and whether or not this was in fact our child. The truth was, it really did not matter what Camila's condition was. God alone knew who was supposed to be in our family. As we began to pray, we also made the decision not to base the very important decision of who would be our child in our own hands. God alone knew. It was a hard surrender to lay down the expectations of what we hoped to have in a child. We had not planned to adopt a child with severe special needs, if in fact Camila did. What did God have planned? It was very difficult to clear our minds and bring ourselves outside of our own fearful thoughts and what we considered to be our own personal capabilities.

Danny and I decided, through advice from our adoption agency, to have an International Adoption physician review her file. The doctor thought that the seizures could have been febrile seizures (seizures from a high fever, which are very common in children) since there was no information in the file about how many seizures there were. We weren't sure how accurate the measurements and weight were. The file was around 6-8 months old, but the doctor was concerned about her size even when she had been at that age. Camila was tiny. The physician told us that her head circumference was below even the lowest normal range for a child that age. That could be a sign of retardation.

I personally began to read God's Word in a new light. I was finding that God seemed to work on a different plane than our mere human comforts and abilities. It began to become more and more obvious to me that the Lord seemed to find great pleasure, and receive great glory, in taking the least likely person for a task and using that person far beyond their own personal borders, far beyond what they thought possible or could have ever expected. It seemed to be the equation that the Lord preferred in His Word, and no doubt, thus far in my life, now that I looked back and thought on it. God seemingly was always beckoning me outside of my own realm into a complete dependence on Him. It actually made good sense. If I could accomplish life, miracles, deliverance, and peace on my own, there never would have been a need for a Savior. I couldn't though. Obviously, the Lord desires to use people in His limitless realm of capabilities, and not their own personal realm of possible.

I began to dwell on the thought that God just might be beckoning us into an unknown area. An area that would demand, once again, complete dependence on Him. As Danny and I prayed about sweet little Camila, we began to question our perspective on life, and what real surrender meant. What if God wanted us to lay aside our own personal expectations in order to allow Him to lead us directly to our child, even if it didn't appear to be what we had previously expected?

We believed God could do way more than we ever could think or imagine. As we prayed, we began to feel a rising of faith within us. We had an assurance and a peace that Jesus was leading us to step out and request this little girl who was outside our approved age range, by Peru, and possibly outside our approved special needs range by the United States government, as well.

I called our agency and asked them what would happen if we went ahead and requested little Camila. What would Peru's response be? If the Peruvian adoption authorities said no, what would it mean to our approval to adopt a child from Peru? Anything at all?

Our agency made it clear that they had never had anyone request a child outside of their given approval range. They were uncertain as to how Peru would respond. Others we knew who were familiar with Peruvian adoption thought perhaps Peru would not look favoringly upon us disregarding their given approval. Some kindly advised us not to do it. We were sure there must be a way to respectfully request a child by expressing that we believed we were a good match for that particular child, even if we were formerly given different restrictions. We prayed and prayed some more.

Our agency did a little research and finally let us know that they would advocate for and support us if we wanted to go ahead and request Camila! They were very up front that it was not likely that Peru would match us with Camila, considering the fact that we were basically asking for something they already told us we could not have. Our agency wanted us to be prepared for the worst case scenario. They also wanted us to be aware that most of the time in a normal Peruvian adoption process, Peru doesn't match a family with the first child they request. It is considered normal for it to take two or possibly more requests before Peru approves a match. While this information wasn't pleasant to hear, we focused more on what we believed was the Lord leading us forward through the impossible once again. We were relieved and overjoyed to have our agency supporting us in this endeavor.

We began to work on a letter of request for sweet little Camila, who was from Iquitos, Peru, in the Amazon jungle. It was all strangely ironic. The Amazon was the one region that I had doubted we would travel when we were learning about Peru in the beginning. I had no reason for that doubt, but remembered reading about all of the different parts of Peru and thinking of where we might end up going. I read about malaria and dengue, and the other diseases found in the Amazonas regions, and felt assured that we would never possibly be going to one of those areas. I was confident we'd end up in the highly traveled Cuzco area, or perhaps in Lima itself. What if we actually did end up going to Iquitos, Peru, which was the birthplace of Camila?

We could feel the expectation and hope rising up within us. It was very timely, because we were so weary of the wait. It didn't take us long to formulate a letter of request. Danny and I wrote it as humbly as we knew how, asking Peru for permission to move forward with adopting Camila. We gave numerous reasons why we believed we would be a good family and a good home for Camila. We ended our letter with the following:

We are confident that Camila would be the best child for our family, and we are committed to be being the best family for her. We respectfully request the honor and privilege of parenting her, and we are committed to loving and caring for her as our very own child.

Thank you,

Danny and Calley Reed

The letter was sent to Peru to be translated. After about two weeks of translation, the letter was delivered to the central authority for adoption in Peru. We had hopes that we might be presented at that same month's consejo (matching meeting, where waiting children are matched with waiting families). The consejo was held once a month, and we began praying for quick resolve for our request.

Unfortunately, a longer wait was ahead. Peru responded to our letter of request for Camila. They told us that our letter of request was "touching," but we needed to show further proof of our ability to care for her.

The adoption authorities of Peru wanted us to go back and do a new work up on our finances. We had to do another interview with a social worker that proved us able to care for a child so close to Amaus' age, and our financial ability to tend to a child who could possibly have special needs. They also wanted us to get the same psychologist who had interviewed us before to review Camila's file and write a report telling Peru that we were able to care for her and our youngest son Amaus, considering that they were so close in age.

The psychologist wrote an amazing letter that obviously took time and effort and didn't even charge us for it. He reiterated over and over that we were capable of attending to another child.

When all of the new requested paperwork was completed, it was finally sent to Peru. We waited on the information to be translated and then it was finally submitted to the adoption authorities of Peru to await reviewal.

Chapter 11

In Spite of Everything

All of our family began to get excited about Camila. My Meme and aunt went shopping for little girl clothes, since we had a roundabout size for her. They gave us a stack of adorable little goodies for Camila. It was so exciting to have people standing in faith with us.

One day I had a good heart to heart with my Meme about Camila, as we sat on stools across from each other at her kitchen counter. I expressed to her our concerns about not fully knowing Camila's needs or condition, but that we were simply praying and trusting God's direction.

My Meme, who is one of the strongest and hardest working women I have ever known, had never been a typical grandma or person, for that matter. She was a carpenter, always teaming up with the menfolk to put shingles on a house, or helping build churches on mission projects. She could build just about anything she decided she'd like for her house, or for someone else. Shortly after Danny and I were married, he had been astounded to learn that my Meme climbed a huge tree to get a baby squirrel for a grandchild to bottle feed. However, she also was incredibly beautiful woman who was fashionable and also a great cook! But besides being what I consider to be super woman, she also happened to have a lot of experience with these issues of children and surrender. As I spilled my heart out to her that day in her kitchen, she gave me one simple bit of advice that I'll never forget. She looked at me with the same watery eyes I had over the seriousness of the matter.

"Calley," she said. "There's one thing I know for sure. If this is God's will for you, then everything is going to be alright."

I knew she was right. I knew she knew this fully herself and could say every ounce of it from a place of surrender that she had lived out most of her life.

My Meme had once been a young mother of three small children when a family member had birthed a set of very sick twin babies. One of the babies died immediately after birth, but the other twin, Mary Ann, was born with severe cerebral palsy. When the family member decided they could not take care of the child, it became a family dilemma. As everyone held up their hands in wonder of what would happen to Mary Ann, my Meme's father approached her. "Julia Ann," he had told her that day. "You need to take that baby and raise it as yours." My meme responded the only way she knew how. "Yes sir."

From that day forward she and my Papa had cared for Mary Ann as their own. Mary's condition required constant care and patience, and a lifelong commitment of surrender was lived out without question or complaint after that day of responding, "Yes sir," to a need that she and my Papa had willingly answered.

My heart began, even with some reluctance and fear, to say "Yes sir" to whatever the Lord was calling us to do. No matter the condition, no matter the cost, God would lead us forward and everything was going to be alright. Our prayers at home began to change again.

Lord, please protect Camila. Please bring her home to us soon. May she feel loved and safe in your hands today..."

We waited every day for any tiny morsel of news from Peru. Anything would have been nice! That they were reviewing things...that they were presenting our request at the next consejo...anything! Soon, though, the August consejo was held and our family was not presented that month after all. I scanned the results from the matching meeting in a frenzy, checking to see if Camila had been matched with another family. That could always be a possibility. My heart let out a huge sigh when I saw that she was not matched at the August consejo.

Early in September we received big political news from Peru. A new president had been voted into office. No one in the adoption realm knew for certain what the new president would mean for foreign adoption, as each new governmental leader typically implemented new ideas, rules and changes. It was only a little later when one change took place on the adoption front. The new president had appointed a new minister of adoption. The next word came as a heavier blow to all families waiting on news from Peru. All adoption requests and consejos were placed on hold, while the new adoption director diligently went through information, checked on children, and got familiar with the children on the Peruvian Priority Adoptions list. She would not hold another consejo until she had thoroughly checked on things. This was good news, as a whole. But sad news for those families like us. We had now been waiting over a year and a half to bring our child home from Peru.

September, one of the longest months of my life, came and went with no word from Peru. Not our agency, nor our in-country representative had any clue as to when another consejo would be held.

Since the consejos were always held at the end of the month, we could easily say that now we at least had to wait until the end of October, and possibly longer, before we were able to hear any response about our request. We buckled down in our stance of faith and continued to pray for Camila.

All that I could do was stand on the Word of God. It was all I had. I was learning that it was all that I needed. Deep inside, I was very weary of the waiting. In my flesh, I often thought that if we were not approved to adopt Camila, I just wanted to quit. I really would not be able to go on, I was sure. I came to points in myself of just desiring to wash my hands and end the madness. But I knew I couldn't do that. Not with my precious child waiting for her mommy and daddy to come and finally bring her home. I hung tightly to the one thing I knew at the time. I knew, with everything in me, that Jesus had directed us all of the way. I knew He alone had awakened us in the middle of our contentment and pointed the way that He wanted us to go. And as certain as I was of Jesus' leading, I was certain of one other driving truth. I knew that I would be disobeying my Lord if I decided to quit. That was something I would never be able to live with myself for doing. I just didn't have anything left in me, it felt. The road had been much longer and harder than I had ever expected. But as hard as it had been, I had never been alone.

October brought a little more peace. The days were growing shorter, and the Louisiana weather was growing cooler. I entered a little more rest, and Danny and I continued to wait and pray. I attempted to resign my thoughts to other tasks, like the new year of homeschooling that had recently begun. I dove into those tasks and tried to fix my thoughts there. We also continued doing everything we knew to raise the rest of the money we would be needing. I began making and selling handmade bracelets, which turned out to be a hit. We also began planning yet another garage sale.

When we looked at our finances, it was such a testimony to all that the Lord had already fulfilled. Every penny of the money needed along the way had been provided, up to that point. We were approximately $10,000 away from paying for everything in an estimated $30,000 adoption process. It was truly awing to look back and see all of the ways that God had provided! We prayed for God to reveal to us where the rest of the needed money was, and how he wanted us to go about getting it.

The days got shorter and cooler, and with them came some of the fun things our family enjoys together each and every year. During October in our town along with a neighboring town, a hot air balloon race and festival are held. It is always a fun time our kids really look forward to. There are fireworks, flea markets, and carnivals. It isn't uncommon for hot air balloons to land near our home, and throughout the weekend they are constantly flying overhead.

It has become tradition for us to load up the boys early on Saturday morning of the balloon races and run to the levee, which borders the Mississippi river, to catch the first race. We usually bring a quilt and have breakfast while we watch the balloons. We eat breakfast, watch the races, and take turns rolling down the steep levee in our own races. Sometimes balloons land right beside us on the levee top as we enjoy our breakfast picnic.

In 2010, the first balloon festival after we had begun the adoption process, we were sitting on the levee enjoying the sights. On that balloon race morning, a year and a half before, a very memorable conversation with my oldest son, Josiah unfolded. We both sat that early morning on our quilt and discussed with glee the fact that by the following balloon festival, we would have our little girl there to enjoy it with us. We had laughed and joked about how much she would probably love it. We wondered together if she would like to roll down the levee and run with her brothers, and we chatted about whether she'd enjoy the fireworks.

It was now October of 2011, and we were, once again, sitting in our spot on the levee watching hot air balloons over a biscuit breakfast. Josiah and I looked at one another, and I could quickly see by the expression on his face that he was remembering our conversation from the previous year, just as I was.

I said, "Well, we sure thought our little girl would be with us for this year's balloon festival, didn't we? I wish she was here."

Josiah replied to my amazement, with tears in his eyes, "But why isn't she here mama? Why isn't she home yet? I don't understand why it's taking so long! I really wanted her to be here." I gulped and did my best to help him wrap his mind around what I struggled with wrapping my own brain around.

76

It was hard to know what to say when questions like this came up. I certainly had the same questions. Josiah was praying fervently for his little sister, and so was Isaac. Both of them were growing weary and having great difficulty figuring out why their sister still wasn't home yet. We would assure them the best we knew how, that we knew that God was in control of the situation, and that everything was going to come through at the perfect time.

When October 28th rolled around, we assumed that there would not be a consejo, yet again. Our agency had been given no word on the subject, and there was only one business day left in the month. The consejo was never held at the very last day of the month. So we swallowed our expectations and set our hopes that possibly a consejo would finally be held in November.

On Sunday, October 30th, our family left church on a Sunday afternoon and drove out to my dad and step-mom's house for a day of lunch and visiting. While on our way, I received an email on my phone. The subject title slapped me in the face. "Consejo was held October 27!"

I hollered the title through the van, talking in my super excited, speedy squirrel voice that I often break out when I am overly thrilled and anxious.

I proclaimed it again through the van, "There was a consejo on Thursday! There was a consejo on Thursday! Oh my gosh!" The email was from an adoption group I am a part of that watches the Peruvian adoption site and posts the consejo results each month. The email said,

Congrats to the Villa Hope and Lifeline families who were matched at this month's consejo!

Our family was a Lifeline family! I really began to flip out, because we knew of no other family within our agency who was adopting from Peru and had recently requested. Was it us?

I told Danny everything as I clicked on the link to the results. I scrolled to the bottom, where I found our little girl listed! We had been matched! We had been matched! Despite our previous approval! Despite everything! Camila was to be our daughter!!!

I screamed, "We were matched!! Oh my goodness!! We were matched!" The boys began cheering in the back seat, "Camila is our sister! Camila is our sister!" I looked over to see Danny with tears streaming down his cheeks. I also was crying. We had been matched. We were going to Peru! We were going to the jungle!!

The very next day, I called our agency with loads of questions. Basically, they all summed up to, "How long will it be before we can go get our daughter?"

We were required by Peru to write yet another letter stating we accepted the match that we had requested. Seems funny, but true! The letter was completed immediately, and we filled out some other disclosure forms. Basically, documents that verified that no one could predict an adopted child's true state or needs, and no one knew for certain what was in an adopted child's history. We were assuming full responsibility for our decision to move forward with adopting Camila. We printed and signed the important papers and over-nighted them to our agency.

Our agency assured us that it would be a minimum of six weeks by the time we finished filing the I-800 with United Stated Citizenship and received their needed approval. It was the final thing we were required to do before traveling. We had already received approval from USCIS to adopt from a Hague Convention country; now we were required to seek approval to adopt a specific child. If everything went according to the normal timeline, we could be traveling to Peru over Christmas!

We gathered up all of Camila's file information in it's entirety and also began working on filling out the paperwork. Sometimes it felt as though the paperwork would never end.

78

Seeing a light at the end of the tunnel made it easier.

Chapter 12

Uncertain Circumstances, Unwavering Direction

While we worked alongside our agency to prepare those documents, we had a very unexpected thing happen. Something we had not prepared ourselves for, in the middle of all of the wonder and excitement. One Friday night we were at Wal-Mart with our entire crew, when I had a blocked call show up on my cell phone. I didn't know of anyone I had blocked, but also was unsure about who it could be, so I didn't answer. A few minutes later I got a call from our representative at the agency. She spoke in the message in a slightly concerned voice. The message said that our agency had received some updated health information about Camila from Peru that we needed to review immediately. I was supposed to call our rep back right away, yet I couldn't since the number didn't show up. It was the longest ten minutes of my life as I hoped and prayed that the phone would ring again. My head and heart were spinning all at once as I paced up and down the cat food aisle of the store with the kids following behind me. What information could this be?

As time seemed to stand still, I began to have serious fear build up in my mind. What a strange thing fear is! Gone one minute and rapping on the door beckoning my attention once again!

My mind drifted. What if something terrible had happened? What if they tell us something, and we will not be able to adopt Camila? What if this new health information changed everything?

Finally, the phone rang again as we still were finishing up shopping. I waited with baited breath as our representative explained to me that Peru had required Camila's orphanage to have an updated health check and evaluation done of her. The psychologist who did the update had already sent the information. Our representative then explained, "Please pray about all that you read. If you feel this updated information is reason to change directions, we will understand and support you in that decision." Essentially, this would be the time to speak up or forever hold your peace.

I wanted to break down right there in the middle of Wal-Mart. What was this new information? Why did this even have to happen? We left in a hurry, and I forgot about groceries and bedtimes and dashed straight for the laptop where I immediately downloaded the updated file information.

I was baffled at first as I began reading. Nothing had been changed on her information, not even her weight and height, which was approximately eight months old on the first report we received. Why was it all the same now, nearly an additional four to six months after it was submitted to the adoption authorities. This was an update?

Then I found one word changed throughout the file. Everything else was nearly exactly the same as it had been before. Everywhere that it had said "Severe developmental delay" before, it now said, "SEVERE MENTAL RETARDATION" in the biggest letters I think my heart had ever read. There was no proof of any new testing or any new reasons for this diagnosis. I was so confused as to how absolutely nothing could have changed on information that was nearly a year old, and why in the world Camila was now thought to be severely mentally retarded.

Danny read the information over my shoulder as I scanned through it once again. There was silence from both us. Then I felt the need to try to explain it away and try to assure myself and Danny that this just couldn't be right. It just couldn't. I was grasping for explanations, though, and fumbling. I had nothing. Nothing to go on and no way of knowing what Camila's true condition was. I finally gave up in the fallacy of my stuttering and began to weep. Danny also began to weep.

There was nothing either of us could say that night. We both felt lost in the heaviness of our emotions and the reality of what we had just read. Our thoughts, however, were written all over our distressed faces.

I'll never forget the empty feeling that consumed me as Danny went to bed in silence, refusing to speak about it anymore. I sat up in the recliner and wept. I crumbled to pieces in the light of this information that could very certainly be a reality. I wept because I wondered if we had been wrong. I wept because I wondered if we had been right. I wasn't sure what was right and what wasn't. If we moved forward with this adoption, what would it mean for life as we knew it? If we didn't move forward, how could we go on; especially after all of the ways that the Lord had miraculously confirmed our steps?

As I sat up that night by myself, in a rare silence only found at bedtime with a house full of children, I began to remember. I began to remember our prayers when we requested precious Camila at consejo, and how we had undoubtedly, whole-heartedly trusted the will of the Lord to be done in that matching meeting. I remembered us praying, fasting, and crying out fervently for the Lord to direct our steps. I remembered us knowing without a shadow of a doubt that the Lord had brought to pass a great miracle when we were matched against all odds with a child outside of the age Peru had previously told us we could adopt.

What had changed now? I asked myself that over and over as I sat up that night in solitude, bearing the weight of our shocking news. What was different about God's will now?

Would the Lord call us to something that He wouldn't equip us for? Was God surprised now that this information was sent to us? Was God even surprised by Camila and her exact condition? What had changed in regards to how God had directed us? I could not deny that nothing at all had changed and that the same God who had called us forward already knew what we would find out that night.

Before I laid my head down to rest, I had settled a few issues in my heart. We either had meant it when we said that we trusted the will of the Lord to be done in that matching meeting, or we didn't. I knew in my heart we had meant it with everything in us, and I knew we desired God's will to be done beyond any other thing. When the road appeared simple, it was easy to say I trusted Jesus. Now that my expectations had been shattered, did I still trust?

There were a good many inconsistencies in this new file that raised a lot of questions in my mind about its accuracy. For one, no other information had really been updated. We had been able, through our agency, to acquire directly with the caregiver at the orphanage and ask about Camila before this supposed update arrived. We were told she spoke a handful of words and used the potty during the day, only wearing a diaper at night. We were also told that she laughed and responded to affection. This did not sound like a severely mentally retarded child to me.

Another strange thing was in this recent file we had received, it said that Camila still struggled with walking. We knew something wasn't right there because we had miraculously happened upon a blog of two college age girls who were volunteering at Camila's orphanage. They had blogged about Camila and how difficult it was to keep up with her because she would take off running. This raised more serious questions. Why would the information be this inaccurate? Was someone wanting to convince us not to adopt Camila? It was hard to know how to sort out the lack of information and understand what was really going on.

The next afternoon, when Danny finally arrived home from working on his Sunday sermon at the church, we had an afternoon cup of coffee and a good long talk. I had felt like I was hanging on pins and needles all that morning because I was wondering what in the world was actually going on in Danny's mind about everything. I wondered if he had come to the decision for us to dissolve stepping forward with the adoption. It was a morning of teetering and wondering. If Danny had made the decision to not continue forward, I undoubtedly just wanted to quit entirely. I wanted to be through. I couldn't bear the thought of living anymore in false hopes and constantly dissolved dreams. I thought, if Danny believes we are wrong about Camila then we had to have been wrong about everything.

But that afternoon over coffee, I wondered why I had ever assumed Danny wouldn't be in tune with me. He had also walked the same long road that I had walked. As a family, we had walked it together.

Danny put it simply. "I know in my heart if we refuse this little girl, we will regret it forever. I know we will be sinning. This just isn't some name on a list anymore...this is the child we have accepted as our daughter."

We went on to discuss the possibilities and what it might be like to adopt a child who was severely mentally retarded. My mind continually went back, though, to all of the inconsistencies in the file. As I stared at the pictures we had of Camila, I also doubted this diagnosis. She was a bright eyed, beautiful and focused child, who clapped her hands in her pictures. It was not the photograph of a severely mentally retarded child. But regardless, Danny and I once again came to the conclusion that we would fully accept Camila, even if our hopes were unfounded and the diagnosis was accurate.

We were required to write up an affirmation that we still wanted to continue with the adoption in light of the recent information. We had that affirmation ready first thing Monday morning, and scanned and mailed it to the agency.

Before long, we finished preparing documents for USCIS. We mailed the packet of information to US Citizenship and another wait began. After a couple of weeks, I called to check on progress. Unfortunately, I received the disappointing news that nothing had really been done yet. But the following week, our adoption agency was contacted by the person who would be our officer at USCIS. The officer did not have good news.

According to our agency's conversation with the officer at USCIS, the lady who had been assigned to our case seemed to be very "by the book." Because of the recent file update that was sent to us from Peru, this officer believed Camila's needs were considered outside of our original CIS approval, which was based on our first home study. Our first home study had given us an approval for one to two children with normal to moderate special needs. This word, "severe" threw things into a different category. Our CIS officer believed we would have to do more updating on our file. We weren't sure what that would entail, but we waited as the officer consulted with her supervisor to find out.

When we finally heard back from CIS through our agency, we couldn't believe our ears. The officer reported to our adoption agency that we would have to update our entire home study. That essentially would entail calling our local social worker to come to our home again and update the huge home study she had done nearly two years prior. She had to assess our family and find out if she thought we were able to take care of a child financially and physically, who could potentially have severe special needs. These new updates would also cost more money. We also would have to go back to Jackson, Mississippi, to redo the biometric fingerprints.

Our agency told us that this particular CIS officer had serious questions and concerns about our ability as parents to take care of our three small children along with a child who could potentially have severe special needs....not to mention the financial strain of those potential needs.

The thought of a stern CIS officer meticulously inspecting our finances, psychological reports, and our family dynamics, with a very negative outlook brought new concerns into my heart. Our adoption agency reminded us several times that many people were refused by CIS at this point, and we should be prepared for that possibility. When I let my mind go to the thought that there could be a possibility that CIS would refuse us, it was more than I could bear. What would we do if CIS said we couldn't adopt Camila?

The night that we received the news of this most recent delay, I cried for a good long time. Danny and some friends decided I needed some ice cream therapy! Nothing like a thousand calories to help a gal feel better! We all went out, me with a swollen and red face, and enjoyed some laughing and fellowship. While we drove around that evening, my sister-in-law texted me some words of encouragement that really helped me recognize that I had once again surrendered to fear. Ahh! When would I ever learn to simply trust?

For my thoughts are not your thoughts, nor are your ways my ways...for as the heavens are high above the earth, so are my ways higher than your ways and my thoughts than your thoughts. Isaiah 55:8-9

God didn't need to work this thing out in a way that matched my human understanding. In fact, He could pave a way that was completely invisible to my mere human vision. What looked dooming and hopeless in my eyes, looked so different in the eyes of Him who loves to place the fatherless in families. He could work out a path that was above anything I could perceive or feel cozy in. The situation that appeared so scary and unknown to me, was a great opportunity for God to reveal His glory, and confirm His plans to us all over again. And who was I to rob Him of the glory He was due? He could show it in any way He so decided, and I only needed to let Him work.

Faith slowly began to rise from the depths again. I remembered that we wholly trusted God when we requested Camila, and how the Lord had worked out everything, against all odds. I stood on that miracle. I was looking back as the Israelites were told to look back and not forget the things God had done to deliver them from the hand of the Egyptians. The more I looked back at the miraculous things that I had seen God do, the less afraid I was of a pessimistic CIS officer. Faith grew as my thoughts shifted from thinking on the trial at hand, to focusing on the battles already won.

Danny and I took a deep breath and got to work on a new arduous list of tasks that the US government was now asking of us. It turned out that all of the updates would end up costing a pretty good chunk of money. Updating the home study meant paying the social worker to do the work, and we would have to also complete all of the state requirements for updating a home study. This consisted of updating any state requirements that were over a year expired. We all had to complete the processes of new health physicals as well as state and federal fingerprints. This had nothing to do with the other biometric finger prints that we were going to be required to update.

We got to work. Our social worker, who was super, came the very weekend we called her. She worked speedily on the update and we began scheduling our various appointments. We traveled from one end of the state to other for fingerprinting and prayed for state back-ground checks to arrive in a hurry. Our boys were worn out with tests and travel! That's for sure!

Chapter 13

Beautiful Provision

God continued to provide all of the money we needed for each expense that we faced. My mother-in-law Betty had been busy painting beautiful and unique textured paintings to sell at an art sale to help us raise money for travel to Peru. She planned out the sale and also a flea market for a fundraiser. A sweet friend who sold jewelry also planned a party to help. We began planning another barbecue chicken dinner sale. All of those things enabled us to be yet one step closer to having the finances we needed to make our travel to Peru a reality.

One day I went out to the mailbox. It was about a month before Christmas and inside I found a Christmas card. The front of the card said, "Merry Christmas across the miles!" And someone had drawn an airplane flying in the clouds that were already on the picturesque card. On the plane was written "Air Peru." Inside was "Merry Christmas" in block letters. There was $500 cash inside. I was in complete tearful shock that day at the mailbox with the sudden realization of what a precious gift it was to be a part of the Body of Christ. It truly was such an inspiring and humbling thing to have so many people praying for and supporting us. It reminded us constantly of the goodness of the Lord and His beautiful active church.

Another family that we had gotten to know throughout our adoption wait, who also was in the process of adopting from Peru, sent us a Christmas card with $100 inside. We were in awe of their giving to our family, as they themselves were paying for an adoption just like we were.

More money began to come in like this, sometimes anonymously. We had friends give us nearly $1000 after someone gave them a large part of that money and told them to bless someone else with it. We had friends who had been in a worship band that no longer played actively together. The band decided to donate their last $700 to our adoption.

Things like this happened frequently. We never got used to it. It brought us to our knees in thanksgiving and awe of God at work through His people. It was always right on time and money began to collect in our adoption account to cover the travel expenses that we knew would be forthcoming. The best I could figure, with the cost of plane tickets for our entire family, including my step-mom who would be going along to help us, we would be spending somewhere to the tune of $12,000.00 to travel to Peru, stay a month, and complete the last bits of the adoption. It was absolutely miraculous to see God provide abundantly beyond our wildest imaginations.

Our social worker finally finished updating our home study and we were able to get all of the other required updates sent to CIS. Gathering all of those updates had delayed us significantly, and it quickly became apparent that we would not be making it to Peru for Christmas, or even for the New Year for that matter.

I went about decorating our home for the holidays, as usual. I made our Camila her own stocking, and we all had our minds on Peru as we celebrated with our normal Christmas festivities. We were rejoicing about the good things we undoubtedly believed were on the way, yet felt slightly disappointed at the most recent delays. We had so longed to have Camila in our arms and at home with us for Christmas, but we were really trying our best to remember that God had his reasons for these delays. On Christmas morning we prayed at breakfast for the Lord to bring Camila home quickly. Danny gave me a beautiful charm with Camila's name to add to my necklace that included our sons names. It was beautiful.

After all of our documents were submitted, I became the most frequent caller to the CIS offices that they'd probably ever seen. I couldn't stand it. I had to call at least weekly to check on progress. They got to know me and would chuckle when I made yet another check on our documents.

One day when I called, they asked me for the typical information. Then they proceeded to give me our officer's name. It was supposed to be the name of the officer handling our case. The only thing was, it wasn't the officer we had been given to begin with.

I asked, "Wait. This wasn't the officer we had previously. Do you guys normally change officers in the middle of a case?" The person who answered the call said, "No, but the officer you had before will be working in another department now, so you were assigned a new officer."

This immediately felt fishy to me. Fishy in a good sort of way, that is. It was the same scenario when Peru requested new information because they doubted our physical and financial ability to care for Camila. We had gotten to work on their list of requests and then suddenly someone new was in charge in the middle of our documents being reviewed! Soon after that, we discovered we were matched with Camila!

Here we were, finally finishing up a long list from CIS from our very meticulous officer who had serious concerns about our ability to care for Camila. We had been taking care of the things asked of us, and then suddenly got news that the officer would no longer be handling our case. How strange. Could the Lord be showing us that He will do whatever He needs to do to bring His plans to pass in the life of a surrendered believer? It was too identical to the previous issues and delays we had had with Peru for us to merely count it a coincidence. What was God up to?

Surprisingly, our new officer was the most delightful person we had talked to at CIS. She seemed to be working on our case as quickly as she possibly could. But no doubt, even with her speed, we were quickly approaching March of 2012, and still had no idea when we would finally be able to go to Peru.

Chapter 14

Boundless Capabilities

I t was crazy the way our family life would always take a punch after Danny and I came to a place of choosing to trust God in faith regarding a situation or trial. As soon as we planted our feet in God's Word, determined to be undeterred by an opposing circumstance, we would undoubtedly have the worst time with disobedience and all out chaos would break out in our home following that stance of faith! It became predictable. Danny and I both knew that when we decided to believe God over a situation, things were about to crank up a notch. It was coming. Like clock work, when we were having to bear down and cling to God's Word with every ounce of strength we had remaining, the things that all of our skeptics had questioned in our parental ability would become a reality. We could have four great weeks of living, all three of our sons doing excellent in school and playing well together. And then Boom! Like our children had overheard one of those skeptical comments from SNA in Peru, or even USCIS's recent questions to us that showed they doubted our ability to take care of another child. They would suddenly feel the need to respond to those questions by displaying terrible behaviors and serious demands. It would be a real temptation for us to give way to fear again, and wonder if these "powers that be" were right after all. What if this all really was too much for me? For our family?

But as we chose to stand in faith on what we knew to be God's will, we found the behaviors too subsided, often in a matter of minutes. The change usually came when we finally recognized their root. After all, Satan is real, active, and desires to derail every plan that God has set in motion, and the only way he can possibly achieve that is by discouraging God's children by simply causing them to doubt what God has said. If Satan could use government authorities to claim we were incapable, and then sway daily circumstances to make us feel incapable, he could succeed in causing us to stop believing what God had plainly said. If he succeeded, one more child would remain an orphan, and more than likely, never come to know the redemption found in Jesus Christ.

Truth be told, it didn't really matter what I felt capable of on those terrible days of heaving and hoeing in waves of doubt, as I struggled to breathe and stand in faith. What mattered was what God had said. God did not call our family to adopt based on our ability. He called us based on our surrender. And I knew that according to His word, He doesn't work along the lines of our capabilities. When we are truly surrendered to His plans, and believe Him for them to come to pass, we see His results. His capabilities are boundless. They are endless. There is no end to what the Lord alone can do. When we step into faith, we step out of our simple, limited human capabilities and step into the capabilities of the Almighty God. There are no limits in that realm.

So I knew it. God had made it plain. I could do whatever He called me to, and by golly, I could do it with victory! After all, if Jesus asks us to rejoice in all things, that must also mean while we are waiting and trusting Him. And if He asks us to then it's certainly possible.

During this hard wait, we received another beautiful confirmation that no doubt was directly from Jesus. Danny and I had known a friend for years who attended another church in our area. We frequently saw her and visited with her at different church gatherings and events. Earlier in our adoption process, I was visiting at a baby shower with her, when I found out that she was from Peru; Something I had never known before. "What a neat coincidence," I thought. We had discussed the fact that she was from Iquitos (which didn't mean anything to me at that time, nearly a year earlier). She had also mentioned that several of her family still lived there, and that her aunt did something dealing with adoptions in Peru. Again, I thought, "How crazy!"

Now that we had been matched with Camila, who was in Iquitos, Peru, we began communicating with our friend more and more. She and her husband, along with another friend, came over and ate supper with us. We had a neat time discussing Peru. She brought along some delicious Peruvian food for us to try. We knew right after tasting it, that if all Peruvian food was that delicious, we were in for a treat!

Soon after, we began discussing the fact that we would be going to Iquitos as soon as we received the okay from CIS. She connected us with an awesome missionary couple there, who we began messaging online. They were such an encouragement to us as well. This missionary couple offered to help us in any way while in Peru, serving as translators, or taking us to and from the airport.

One day Joyce, our friend who was from Iquitos, called with the most amazing news. Her aunt actually worked at the exact orphanage that was housing our Camila! Now this was just nuts. Of the over 520,000 estimated orphans in Peru, we had requested a little girl from the same town as a friend that only lived a couple of miles away. On top of that, her aunt was the administrative assistant at the exact orphanage! The world suddenly felt so incredibly small! Rather, it made me realize how small it was for a great big God to work with. What in the world can He not bring together and orchestrate? Nothing is too hard for Him!

I had to call everyone I knew and share this completely crazy thing God had done! There was absolutely nothing coincidental about this. God alone could give us this connection. When we called to share this with our agency, I think they had a hard time believing it. It was just that nuts.

It was so brilliant...this landscape the Lord was painting right before our eyes. The way the colors began to blend together. It was like a magnificent water color flowing seamlessly in breathtaking colors. With each stroke of our Master's hand, things became a little more clear to us. When we first stepped out based on God's word to our family in regards to adoption, all we had was a mere sketch, a dim outline, rather, of where we were going and why. At times, things didn't even seem to make sense. The strokes that our Master painted seemed blurred to our short-sighted-vision. We couldn't make out the object, or what this creation would eventually become. We couldn't discern what was coming into shape.

I had not wanted to admit my fear in that. But it was so evident, so many times. The thing was, this wasn't just any ol' simple thing we were watching come to pass. It was a huge transformation of my life as I had always known it or ever expected it to be; with all of its previous comforts and all of its walls. When the Lord first planted this adoption seed in our hearts, I felt much like Abram, when God spoke to Him and said, *"Go to the land that I will show you." (Genesis 12:1)*

What was this land we were going to? What would the end result be? My fears caused me to wonder and even doubt at times where God was leading us. Would we go to Peru and bring home a child who had serious and severe physical and mental issues? If so, I wanted to be ready and find joy in that, even though in the true depths of my heart, I was a scared little girl myself, wondering how I would react to such a huge change of direction in my life. I was constantly countering those fearful thoughts, waging war against them, rather. Constantly reminding them that there was one thing that blew every internal fear known to man completely out of the water.

This one constant- this one truth, was that I had made Jesus KING of my life many years back. That's really all that mattered. Either I meant it wholeheartedly, or I didn't. If I did, I had sincerely forfeited my own rights. If I did, I should now consider myself crucified with Christ. And I knew in sincerity, that the life I had laid down was no longer my own. That meant, and had to mean forevermore, that Jesus alone was and is in charge of this life. He can call it, direct it, and lead it however He deems best. It was always easy to say that until it meant coming to a bend in the road where I would have to make a really defining choice. In those hard times of deciding again, I had the privilege of proving or disproving what I had claimed to commit to Jesus, so many years before.

Chapter 15

Gloriously Broken

O ne night, I fought myself in another internal war, as the mystery of where we were going and how this whole thing would end began to weigh so heavily on my mind that I could scarcely stop crying or find peace. As my thoughts finally built to a climax through a Satan led series of what-ifs, I kept having a scripture come to mind faintly in the background of my concerns.

The scripture was from John, and came from the passage where the angel Gabriel comes to Mary and tells her that she will carry the Son of God. Her response kept seemingly singing in my ear all day in the background of my cares.

"Behold the bond slave of the Lord; May it be done to me according to your word." (Luke 1:38)

That night, I had not found real peace. I had honestly never stopped worrying to think on that scripture. As I tucked the boys into bed, Amaus took off running at high speed into Camila's room and grabbed the Bible story book that all three of our sons had bought for Camila with their own combined, saved money. He brought it into his room, and said, "Read this to me, Mama!"

I didn't know where to begin. I'm always a little baffled when I'm handed a novel, dictionary or a phone book by one of my toddlers and asked to read. Where do I begin?! So I did what my typical resolve is. I just flipped open the Bible storybook and picked the first random story.

There before me, as the Lord would have it, was a cartoon drawing of Mary kneeling before the angel Gabriel. The scripture, written so that a toddler could understand said,

"I am God's servant. May what you have said happen to me."

I couldn't stop the tears from flowing because I knew that the Lord had been trying to whisper that scripture to me all day long, yet I had chosen worry and fear instead. But on that night, He had used my youngest son to direct me to the scripture that unquestionably spoke straight to the heart of my level of surrender. It brought me all the way back to my dream of floating through the muddy river and all of the drowning people crying out for help. Was I still too afraid of letting someone into my boat, rather than simply trusting God?

That night, I wept endlessly in thanksgiving. My Lord always met me right in my need. Yes, my baffled three-year-old stared at me and was slightly confused as to why that story had made me cry my eyes out, but that didn't stop the thankful tears.

I cannot remember feeling so gloriously broken, or so joyously free as when I was faced with the knowledge that everything in my world could be flipped upside down beyond recognition...yet it was still worth it to choose that complete surrender, once again. Never have I felt such release as that night that I decided all over again that the Lord knew what He was doing, and there truly was nothing at all to fear in His arms. I knew from walking with Him, that He loved me immeasurably beyond my imagination. I knew that He wanted the very best for me. I knew He had better things planned for me than I could ever dream, and that's saying something for someone like me who is constantly cooking up a new plan or goal. His plans were best. I knew I wanted those plans alone.

The peace rained like a river when this issue was settled. I knew without a shadow of a doubt that He was painting something glorious. Who cares if I couldn't yet make it out? He was beautifully confirming our path in such awe inspiring ways. And I knew from His word that any man or woman who completely surrendered his or her life, plans, and dreams to the hand of the Master was never disappointed. His Word said it so simply, yet so powerfully. *"Whoever trusts in Me will never be disgraced. " (Romans 10:11)*

There were new issues of surrender rising up within Danny and me. Our conversations seemed to run more and more to what real surrender was and if we were truly walking in it. These conversations usually shifted to the one issue neither of us really had the bravery to lay down. It was another one of those internal battles of wonder that left us questioning where God might actually lead us, and what it meant to our five, ten, and fifteen year plans.

Why did we struggle so with entirely laying down our family size to the Lord? I guess it was because it was the generally accepted thought, even amongst the Body of Christ, that while God might call a person to lay down everything in his or her entire life to Him, that one measly issue of how many children a family should have was of very little importance to God. After all, didn't God give people common sense?

As I sought the heart of the Father and what His Word had to say about children, I found over and over again that the popular viewpoint that was accepted culturally was very very far from the picture the Lord clearly laid out in His Word. One day as I was reading the Word and studying on the subject of faith, I was brought back to a scripture that had hit so many times, yet never in this one way.

"For we walk by faith and not by sight." (2 Corinthians 5:7)

Wow. God never did call His children to walk by common sense after all. He never called them to walk according to their comforts. He never called them to walk according to their financial ability. He never told them to walk by what they felt mentally and physically capable of in themselves, either. He simply told them to walk by faith. That means fully trusting and believing Him. Plain and simple.

So how could we doubt anymore that God knew perfectly well how many children needed to be in our family? How could we say we were trusting Him to take this matter into our own hands and prevent pregnancy? What? Were we as believers and followers of the Most High God actually going to create life outside of God's will? Could we actually disrupt God's plans for our lives by trusting Him? What a hilarious thought! Could we bring forth life, the most precious creation by the Lord, without Him who knits children together in the womb, having known about it from the foundation of the world? Absolutely not.

This new idea of surrender was just exactly that. New. It was new to us. Obviously no one knew what we were dealing with in our personal lives, but we just decided to believe what the Lord had made so perfectly clear in His word. He could bring forth life when it was His perfect timing.

Danny and I also knew that if I were to get pregnant, our adoption process would be ended, or at least significantly delayed. We had signed documents at the beginning of the adoption process stating that if we had any idea at all that we were pregnant, we had to inform our agency immediately. They, like most agencies, had a policy of waiting a minimum of a year after a new child was born to continue forward with the adoption process. This policy was simply to ensure that people were certain they wanted to continue with the adoption after already adding a biological child to the mix. For Peru, though, almost indefinitely meant no adoption for several years, if at all, for our family. The adoption authorities there were known for ending many, many adoption processes at the word of a pregnancy or young baby. Many people have found it difficult to adopt from Peru with small children. It just was not a simple country to adopt from, and especially not if the family already had small children.

This was another fear we decided to surrender. Would God contradict His own will in our lives and end our adoption process by bringing forth life at the wrong time? What an absurd thought. We were confident, and how could we not be, that God had shown us clearly His plans for us to adopt from Peru. If we were confident in Him, and confident in His will, there was truly nothing to fear. We rested in that.

A few times I wondered if I might be pregnant, as the weeks rolled by and we waited for the approval from United States Citizenship and Immigration. I, being a birth doula, and just having a interest in the subject of fertility, pregnancy, and birth, knew how these things came to pass. Time and time again, I wondered how I was not pregnant when I knew clearly how my body and these things worked. Time and time again it would soon be confirmed that I was not pregnant. In some moments I wondered, "Maybe God has shut my womb from this point on. Maybe this is the end of me being able to bear children physically." I didn't know what God's plans were in regards to our family size, any more than I knew when we would finally end up in Peru or what our child would be like upon arrival. I chose to trust as we continued to wait.

I often found myself wandering into Camila's room and looking at each little toy, each little dress, and each little trinket and thinking of her with affection. What would she think of her room? What would she think of us? My heart so longed to grab her and make up for all of the love and affection that I was sure she had missed. I couldn't bear the thought of her having no one to sing to, teach, and rock her. I couldn't wait to hold her little body and never let her go. It was all that I could do to not want to just jump on a plane and wait for the resolve on the other side. If only that were possible.

I was love sick, so desperately wanting to love my precious little Peruvian daughter. One day I blogged about this heartsick feeling:

1/14/12

101

If I Could Tell You Anything

If I could tell you anything today, it would be how much I love you, even though we've yet to meet. If I could tell you anything today, it would be how I cannot wait to hold you, rock you, and sing to you... How I cannot wait to be there to kiss your ouchies, and hold your hand.

If I could tell you anything today, it would be how excited I am to run with you, chase you, and play with you. If I could tell you anything today, it would be how I long for the time when I can let you help stir up a cake, color pictures with you, and paint your fingernails; How I cannot wait to show you new exciting places, tell you stories, and teach you the joys of living.

If I could tell you anything today, it would be how much harder and harder it becomes to bind up the love I so desire to be able to pour out on you right now. If I could tell you anything today, it would be that no one has forgotten you, and that a daddy, mama, and three big brothers, living thousands of miles away are coming very soon, as very soon as we are able; how, I cannot wait to hold out my arms to you and embrace all of you. Your laughter, tears, broken story, and your future.

Yes. I will tell you the great measures the Lord went to, to speak to your mommy and daddy, who were in a state of content slumber far, far away. The strength and stamina He miraculously provided, and the long journey, that at times seemed so never ending; the path so steep and winding, that there seemed there might never be a resting point. I will tell you how so many precious people saw the vision of your illusive face, right along with us, and decided to join the fight to bring you home. I will tell you of all of the promises the Lord gave us to stand on so we would not grow weary...so we would keep the faith that one day, you truly would be sitting in our laps, on our shoulders, and in our family. And when you are, oh how full and thankful my heart will be. I will rejoice at seeing our faith become sight. And I will rejoice in the miracles I saw on our journey to you- miracles we would have never been a part of had we not chosen the difficult path of adoption. You, we would have never seen. Yes, you are a miracle... If I could tell you anything today...

These feelings of longing for my child reminded me of how I felt at the end of my previous pregnancies. I would do this same wandering process. Go into their nursery and look at every diaper and onesie and think dreamily of what it would be like to hold and snuggle my own sweet, little newborn. When I felt like my babies should have been born, and that extra week or so would roll by...I would wonder if I would ever have a baby. It really did feel like an eternity.

This adoption, where my little girl had been growing in my heart...was a paperwork pregnancy that was pushing close to two years now. From that first day that God had planted the seed in our hearts two Aprils before, here we were now only a few months from April, and still waiting on an answer from CIS. Such a long pregnancy that I prayed would soon be ending.

Finally, one day at the end of February during one of my routine calls to CIS, I got a much appreciated morsel of news. According to our officer, as soon as one final document was reviewed, our approval would be issued. I cried and rejoiced and shouted when I received the news. Danny had not known that I had just called CIS, and he called right behind me receiving the same news. He cheered on the phone with the CIS officer, who got a good laugh at our family who had been calling at least weekly for four months. I'm sure they were just as glad as we were that there were no longer any reasons for us to be calling their offices!

Against every odd, the Lord had brought the victory. Even with financial questions, our physical ability questioned over and over, and our often negative and skeptical "reviewers"- God was bringing us through to a final "Yes!" I was so overwhelmed with joy.

God did not need things to look like they were in our favor at any point. In fact, it seemed it constantly needed to look like they weren't so that He could show us who was really in charge. I knew that He wanted to teach us so much more about trusting Him, and He had used every phase until this point to teach us that truly believing Him throughout the hardest waits and the worst circumstances still meant coming out victorious. Because when I trust in Him, I am truly never disappointed!

I packed our suitcases and stacked them in our little dining room, expecting someone to call any time and let us know that we were clear to travel. I bought all of us cute monogrammed luggage tags. Josiah had robots on his, and Isaac and Amaus had dinosaurs. They thought those tags were awesome. We talked a good bit with the boys about going to Peru. Man, were they excited! Besides gaining a little sister, they were beyond pumped about being able to travel to the Amazon jungle and see so many amazing creatures that they'd only read about in their science books. Amaus only stated over and over again that he was flying on an airplane. That was the huge attraction for him!

Camila had her own little pink suitcase packed full of dolls, blocks, books and the frilly clothes I had been longing to put her in for months. We were obviously just guessing on a wide range of sizes, but from the file we had that was supposedly updated a year before, she was three years old, yet about the size of an 18 month old. I packed some 2T's, assuming we might need them.

It was now the end of summer in Peru, and we were at the end of winter in Louisiana. It was a little strange packing tank tops and shorts and sunscreen with it being rainy and cold outside at our Louisiana home. The fact that the stores started putting their spring and summer items out ridiculously early really worked in our favor for once. I was able to pick up some much needed summer things for our trip.

I had kept my step-mom, Leslie, and my dad updated throughout the whole process. She was so excited about the adventure ahead, just like we were! So she naturally was one of the first to know that we would finally be leaving, and soon!

She worked on squaring everything away for the high school English class she taught and got her bags packed, as well. My dad, who had planned to go with us from the beginning, was unable to take off work, and so Lee Lee, as the kids called her, would be coming along for the Amazon adoption adventure!

After we received a letter in the mail confirming our approval, we assumed that we would be leaving in a week or possibly two. As it turned out, all of our file information, combined with Camila's, had to be wired to the US Embassy in Lima where they also had to do a final review. While this typically is a much quicker process than the CIS approval, there is still some tedious work to be done to ensure that, one final time, the child who is being adopted is officially abandoned and everything is clear to go. As soon as the United States Embassy in Peru gave us their approval, we would be able to leave.

While we were waiting on this word from the Embassy, I received the most timely email from another adoptive friend. Debbie and her husband Tomi were also adopting from Peru and Tomi was from Lima, Peru. They now lived in the states, but Tomi's parents still lived in Lima. Tomi's parents were actually offering to allow us to stay with them in Lima for a fraction of the cost that we would have been paying to stay in an apartment and for our meals, They had a large home where we would have plenty of space to ourselves, if we needed it, once Camila was in our care. This was a huge Godsend. Danny was going to be traveling back to the states one week ahead of me, and he felt so much better about me staying with a kind family than in some apartment alone. The Ardiles family had a housemaid, which is very common amongst the middle class in Peru. She would cook all of our meals. We could not have asked for a more suiting or blessed arrangement!

We were on pins and needles as we waited to get word that the final reviewal at the US Embassy was taken care of. While we waited, we loaded our suitcases with goodies for our missionary friends in Iquitos, and the Ardiles family in Lima. We weighed and re-weighed our suitcases over and over again.

Boy did we have a huge pile of heavy luggage! I could not figure out any other way to pack for a month. I had reduced as much as I knew how! We ended up with five large suitcases and three small carry-ons in the end. I didn't even try to imagine what the scene would look like as we checked this much baggage and rolled through airports with our carry-ons and our boys running around everywhere. I knew that would be quite an experience!

It took about a week for the Embassy to receive the wired file, and then it took approximately one more week for them to review and approve our paperwork. Finally, we were able to book our tickets, at a cost of $9500, to fly to Lima on March 23, 2012. It felt so outside of our element to be dropping that kind of money in one phone call. But God had provided all that we needed to travel to Peru, down to the penny. It was such a miracle and a joy to see that God had confirmed in our lives what He had promised He would. According to our estimates, we had just what we needed to go to Peru and live for a month. Only the Lord could do these things!

Chapter 16

Promises Fulfilled

L eslie met us at our Louisiana home early on the morning of March 23, and we made the drive to Baton Rouge, Louisiana, to catch our flight. Surprisingly, everything ran smoothly. We landed in Houston in time to eat some lunch and prepare for our next flight that would take us the remainder of the trip to Lima, Peru.

After flying out of Houston, we arrived in Lima at 10:30PM. There was a serious bustle of activity as we waited in line at immigration with a slew of carry-ons, jackets, purses and children. I was nervous. I wondered if I'd know what to do and which line to get in, and if I'd be able to communicate with people and a million other things. Amaus was exhausted and he had only just fallen asleep on our long seven hour flight from Houston when we had to wake him up upon landing. When he began to come to, as we stood in line with our multitude of clutter, he began to cry. He began to cry, very, very loudly. Then, we had the most amazing and wonderful first discovery of Peru. Families with small children and senior citizens are always given preference and are ushered to the front of lines so that they don't have to wait!

We were allowed to take a separate line and were quickly pushed through immigration and on our way to claim our baggage. Woo-hoo! We were finally in Peru!!

Although it was late and we all were pretty tired, we were filled to the brim with excitement and expectations. We knew that our in-country rep for our agency, Marisa, would be meeting us after we claimed our bags. We were told to look for a sign with our agency's name and to be aware that there would be hoards of people and signs.

While Leslie, who was an absolute priceless extra pair of hands, held onto one child's hand. Danny took another and they went to claim our mountain of baggage. I assumed the duty of getting our money changed over to Peruvian soles- a task I was extremely nervous about! I found the booth, and thankfully, the fellow working there was fluent in English and very friendly. He helped me get the soles I needed. We would be needing cash over the next few days for taxis, and any other coming and going we would end up doing. I knew nothing about how much everything was going to cost! I pretty much made a shot in the dark on how many soles we needed and went to meet up with our crew.

We pushed two large luggage carts, stacked to the top, and we made our way to the entrance of the airport. The warning we had received was correct. There was a large crowd of people shouting in Spanish that looked to be a mixture of family members searching for other family members, taxi drivers, and only God knows who else, waving hysterically. Finally, I saw Marisa, our rep, and we went and hugged her and introduced ourselves.

Marisa was a delightful, and spunky lady. She was all smiles and full of information and insight as a response to our waterfall of questions and emotions. I could tell we were going to be in great hands in Peru.

The taxi van brought us to the Ardiles' home in the San Borja district of Lima. The home was a beautiful three story, yellow home with a yard completely filled with flowers. The Ardiles were waiting for us with smiles and warm greetings, although it was already pushing midnight. Right off, I knew this family was special. They were embracing and receiving our large family with such warm hospitality and love, although we were complete strangers. It was truly an awing thing to be a part of.

Señor Ardiles was a man who appeared very respectable and kind hearted. He had a raspy kind voice and the sweetest, most giving eyes you've ever seen. Señora Ardiles was a very beautiful and petite woman who spoke with personality and cheer. She seemed to love our sons, and they seemed to take right to the Ardiles' and their home.

The Ardiles didn't really speak much English, so we knew we were in for another treat...being immersed in Spanish while in their home! They led us up a beautiful wooden staircase that was polished until it glistened. We brought all of the luggage up three flights of stairs. We did our best with our broken Spanish, and they, with the bits of English they knew, explained to us where the towels, bathroom, and bedrooms were. The home was just perfect.

Leslie settled into a room with two twin beds and Amaus settled into the bed beside her. Grandmas are always a blast to sleep beside, and Leslie is an expert bedtime story teller! Josiah and Isaac slept in a neighboring room in twin beds, and Danny and I had a room on the third floor. There was a big sunroom on the same floor with many plants and open windows, allowing the Lima breezes to flow in and out.

We quickly realized that there was no air conditioner. We opened the windows and let the breeze blow into our bedroom. As soon as we got comfortable in bed, we realized something else. The city of Lima really came alive at night. I kept hearing some kind of strange music that would come by, along with people constantly honking outside. I wondered if the Ardiles' were just a really popular family, because I couldn't figure out what was up with all of the honking.

The next morning at a delicious Peruvian breakfast of chabata, a yummy crispy bread served with marmalada (jam), we learned that people honk at the intersections to merely let other drivers know they're coming, so they don't have to stop. Pretty hilarious, actually! We also learned several cool facts about the area, through the Ardiles' granddaughter Fiorella who served as a translator. She spoke English well, and she stayed with the Ardiles while attending medical school in Lima.

We felt at home at the Ardiles' house from the very first meeting. They did their best to help us in any way possible. Later in the morning, Señora Ardiles brought us to the neighborhood market. It was an amazing sight for all of us! It was an open air market with heaps of fresh fruits, vegetables, and hanging meat at every turn. There were even little hair salon booths where women and men were having their hair colored and cut. Our kids seemed to be a spectacle at every turn. Women often stopped to pet their heads, and babble something, apparently nice, to them. At first our sons were taken a bit off guard by this reaction. They quickly figured out that other gringo kids were a rare commodity in Peru. They received this response wherever they went.

That evening we met the Ardiles' daughter, Anita and son-in-law Angus, who was from Scotland. We also met two of their children. We hit it off quickly with this friendly family. That evening we went on a van tour of the city and got to walk

110

around some older parts where the architecture was incredible.

Angus was the pastor of an English speaking church in Lima called Union Church. Sunday morning they arranged for us to be picked up, and we really enjoyed the service there. The entire weekend we enjoyed some of the best food known to man. No joke. It was absolutely great in every way! Lots of rice, fresh bread, and potatoes, all cooked in the most unique ways. Ha! What's not to love? There was no meal we did not enjoy to the fullest! Our kids cleaned their plates at nearly every meal.

Sunday night, I had some time to dwell on the huge thing about to take place. In only two days we would finally be meeting our daughter, the little girl of whom we only had two photos. The little Peruvian who we merely had bits and pieces of confusing and contradictory information. One minute my mind was racing one hundred miles a minute about this incredibly large and life-changing event about to take place. The next minute the whole thing felt completely surreal, much like a dream. It didn't even seem real in a way that we were actually sleeping in Lima, Peru, and in a matter of days would be meeting our very daughter. It was such a mysterious, exciting, and gut wrenching feeling, all at once.

The next day, Monday morning, we had to meet with SNA, the adoption authority in Peru. They were to brief us on what to expect when we met Camila. They preferred that we bring all three of our sons with us to the meeting. I was pretty nervous about that. I hoped Amaus, who had been whiny, exhausted and a major handful since we had arrived in Peru, would behave while we sat through this meeting with the SNA psychologists and lawyers who had been so skeptical of our ability to tend to an additional child with our already three small kids. Amaus had pretty much followed in tow with our record over the last couple of years. Every major step of faith, always being followed by tough behavioral issues with our kids. It was a guarantee every time, and he had been quite the handful since we had arrived in Peru, testing the limit at every turn!

Monday morning we had to leave at 7:30AM, and we nervously packed into Marisa's small car and drove to the SNA office. There are no car seat laws in Peru, and seemingly no traffic laws in Lima. We learned a new meaning of aggressive driving as we journeyed through the city.

The appointment at SNA consisted of us meeting in a small conference room with our three children, Leslie, Marisa, two lawyers and an SNA psychologist. One of the lawyers was very straight and to the point. She immediately began inquiring with us about our ability to take care of a child with sever special needs and our other children, as if we had not covered that basis enough already. Then she began to ask us about our financial ability, yes again, to take care of a child with Camila's needs.

Danny and I were a little taken back by the crazy questions, only because we thought we had gone above and beyond what was normally expected of people to prove that we would love and care for Camila. The lawyer's last question to us was, "Are you certain that you still want to adopt Camila?" We both were pretty astounded. "Yes!" was our absolute response, nearly in sync with one another. Had we not wanted to adopt her, why would we be sitting here in Lima with our three sons.

I was so grateful for Leslie during that meeting. When Amaus began to get antsy she was able to take him out for a stroll so we could focus entirely on the interview with SNA.

After all of the questions from the one seemingly stern lawyer, we had to sign some documents that were our official release from Peru to go to the orphanage and continue forward with the adoption process. Then both of the lawyers gathered up all of the folders and documents and bid us farewell. The psychologist stayed on to discuss with us further concerning Camila's upcoming adjustment and response to the overwhelming weeks ahead.

She reiterated over and over that Camila had severe needs, and that she would require much compassion and patience. She warned us that children who are adjusting to adoption often throw tantrums, act out in various ways, and that we should be prepared for a variety of responses. She ended the conversation in near tears, as she told us that she believed that we would be great parents to Camila because anyone who would go through all that we ended up being required to do, surely would love and care for this child. It was reassuring to know that at least this lady believed in us! It was a teary moment for us all. But then again, it didn't take much for me to become an emotional basket case at that point!

When we left the SNA office, it really felt official. We were free now. We were being sent out to finally go and meet our child and proceed with the adoption.

Marisa dropped us off by the Ardiles' home, and we rushed to pack our belongings. I realized right off that some of the things that we had packed weren't going to be necessary in Iquitos, where it was still considered the end of summer. We also had lightened our load slightly by giving the Ardiles' the goodies we had brought for them from the US. It helped some, although it was still a major workout carrying the train of luggage down the three flights of stairs all over again.

We enjoyed one last delicious meal with Señor Ardiles, Señora Ardiles and Fiorella before two large cab SUV's arrived to pick us up with all our many bags.

Our entourage was loaded quickly in the vehicles after we bid farewell to our amazing new friends who had opened their arms to us with such love and hospitality.

When we arrived at the Lima Chavez International Airport, it was a bit chaotic, as we figured out was customary in checking loads of baggage with loads of children. Josiah, Isaac and Amaus chased each other in circles in a small clear area while we shuffled through boarding passes and carry-ons. Leslie, was once again a priceless commodity. She would take care of whatever we couldn't in every moment of need. What a blessing!

We waited at our gate to board the flight to Iquitos- the city that we had been reading about for over six months. Tomorrow, we would meet our daughter. My brain was fuzzy with the seriousness of what was coming to pass. My heart was full with the joys of watching miracles unfold to bring us to Peru. Miracles only Jesus could do. What a very special child Camila must be. God had done so many truly awesome things to bring us to this point, to confirm our steps, and to show He was with us for the entire journey. I sat with tears rolling down my cheeks as my sons sat in a row with their backpacks and snacks. Danny, Leslie and I waited to take our last leg of a trip that had been two years long; a trip that I could have never imagined would have been so challenging, yet had caused our very foundations to rumble in a way that they had needed rumbling. It had been a trip that had caused us to search deeper and find out where we truly placed our trust. Now, here we were, a few hundred miles and less than twenty-four-hours from meeting our very child. The child that the Lord had been directing us to bit by bit, for two years.

A trolley bus soon arrived that took us to board the Peruvian Airline evening flight bound for Iquitos. We were the only gringos aboard the flight, and we received many looks and questions we couldn't answer in Spanish, especially regarding our children. I think the most likely question of them all was, "What is this family possibly doing going to Iquitos with their three small kids?"

We landed in Iquitos at 7:00PM, that evening and we were greeted by a very warm and muggy climate. We went into the airport, claimed our baggage, and stepped out into another small mob of people outside, reminiscent of when we first arrived in Lima, though a much smaller and more casual group. Taxi drivers and family members waiting on loved ones, and people who wanted to help load our baggage for a fee, all swarmed around the small walkway exiting the airport in Iquitos.

A quick look around the parking lot revealed only a small handful of vehicles and all of the taxis were what appeared to be a single motorcycle with a cart attached where the back wheel normally was. The cart or back seat looked like it would hold two or three people at the most. The roof of the backseat carriage reached all the way over the front of the taxi, also covering the driver. Some of the taxis were decorated and airbrushed with different names and sayings on the back. People exited the airport and filled up the moto-taxis, as they were called, with their baggage sitting on the back, in a seemingly unsecured fashion. It was quite a sight!

Having a vehicle was apparently a rare commodity. Our hotel was one of the few at the airport that did, though. We loaded into the van, and a few street children wandered up to us who were evidently looking for some change. This was our first taste of the real needs that the jungle city had.

The streets of Iquitos were dusty and dirty and the air smelled of exhaust, although still thick and extremely humid. Moto taxis were everywhere, and the fact that it was late evening apparently meant nothing to this city. People were everywhere, walking the streets and riding on personal motorcycles. I suddenly felt I had no excuse for never learning to ride Danny's small Honda years back. Especially not when I saw elderly women drive by on their own motorcycles. Whoa! Whole families would be sitting on one single motorcycle. I was not sure that was even possible...and yet, here it was! A dad in front, with two children sandwiched in between, and a mom in back. Moto-taxis filled the streets with no respect for lanes, zooming in and out of traffic and veering to and fro in a very comical way. On our way to our hotel, Marisa pointed as we passed by Camila's very orphanage! Our hearts were bursting within us to know our daughter was sleeping right inside those walls!

When we arrived at our hotel it took us a bit off guard. It was situated in the middle of a very busy row of shops of all kinds. Shops with piñatas hanging, and shops with fabric, shops with medicines, and shops with just about everything known to man. There was garbage and dirt all over the ground. Once we stepped inside our hotel that was squeezed between the slew of shops, we found a beautifully clean hotel decorated with authentic jungle canoes, photographs of the Amazon, and some huge drums made from logs, apparently common to the area. It was a very clean and nice hotel.

Some extremely friendly young men helped us carry our baggage up several flights of stairs to our room on the very top floor. The way it was arranged, it was the only room on that floor. The furniture was simple, but the room was cozy. It had a small kitchenette, bathroom, and two bedrooms.

Leslie, Josiah, and Isaac settled into one room, and Danny, Amaus, and I stayed in the other. I immediately got busy laying out our clothes for the following day. I had no idea what I should wear when going to meet my daughter. I did my best to rest and surprised myself by completely crashing for a night that I expected I'd surely be sleepless. I think that must

116

have been thanks to all of our family and friends praying for us back home.

The next couple of weeks were all slated out for us already. We were expected to make daily visits to the orphanage to see Camila, until the last day, when there would be a going away party for her. Then we would sign the papers that placed her in our custody for the next week. That week was called the family placement week. Two times during the family placement week, a psychologist would visit and check on Camila's progress and how she was attaching to us as a family. If those two visits went well we would sign the official adoption decree on the following Monday morning. The rest of the week we would spend getting Camila's new birth certificate. After that we could fly back to Lima for the last phase of the process dealing with getting Camila's visa from the US Embassy, and her passport, both of which would be required to leave Peru and return home to the United States. This whole process was expected to take four weeks. There was so much that would take place in that time.

We all awoke in dreamy wonder of how our day would unfold. Our hotel had an amazing Peruvian breakfast, Iquitos style. That meant an all out meal with rice, all kinds of meat, fruit, bread and juice. It was fabulous!

We first had to hail two moto-taxis in front of our hotel. Our crew couldn't possibly fit into one. We rode to the local SNA office in Iquitos where we quickly met with a lawyer and a psychologist who also briefed us about our meeting with Camila. They then accompanied us as we hailed three taxis and left for the orphanage.

I couldn't contain myself. Would she be waiting when we arrived at the orphanage? Would we sit somewhere and they would bring her out to us? How was this monumental thing about to come to pass?

When we got out on the street outside of the walled orphanage, I quickly asked Leslie if she'd mind videoing, and

Marisa if she minded taking some photos for us. I wanted to capture every second of this meeting.

Danny, Leslie, Marisa, Josiah, Isaac, and Amaus and I were all led into the orphanage side entrance where we were greeted by a kind orphanage director. We also soon met our friend's aunt, from home. Everyone was very kind to us and some women workers and children from the orphanage watched us from the distance and seemed to be sizing us up. I suppose we did make for a very curious scene!

Danny and I were told to wait in a little sitting area at the center of the orphanage. It was an outdoor pavilion with half walls around it. There was a stool in the corner where Leslie sat with the video camera. The boys sat around her, and Danny and I went and waited on the wooden love seat at the sitting area.

We waited for a few minutes, until we heard a little murmur from Marisa and some of the orphanage workers as they peered in one direction of the property. Danny and I peered over the little half wall, and there, coming our way, was our precious Camila! She held onto the hands of two orphanage workers and peered down at her feet as she walked. She was dolled up in a purple shirt, black leggings, white ruffled socks, and black patent leather shoes.

The orphanage workers stopped and helped her to pick a flower which she carried in her hands. As she walked closer to us, we could make out more of her adorable face and chubby cheeks, her huge brown eyes, and the cutest little smile we had ever seen before. Her hair was cut in what appeared to be bowl cut, and she looked all around as if she was completely clueless as to what was coming to pass. Both Danny and I were crying rivers before we ever even had Camila in our arms.

Camila was brought into the pavilion and was led toward us. She briefly looked at us as she came forward. I picked her up, and she smiled at us for a minute and then began sliding out of our laps in an attempt to get down. When we let her down, she took off running. She threw the flower she had picked up in the air over and over again, smiling and laughing as if it was the funniest thing she had ever seen. Camila ran all over the pavilion. We decided to make a game of it, and we started chasing her. She seemed to love being chased, and she started giggling. I could tell her attention seemed very easily diverted. She would play one little game with us but only be occupied with it briefly, before growing agitated and wanting to run off to something else. I suddenly remembered the goodies I had brought in my bag. Now with bubbles and a large rattle, the games continued.

The boys quickly joined us in the fun and games. They all began competing for Camila's attention and trying to pick her up and hug her. When Camila wanted something, she would make a loud hollering noise and reach for it. If she wasn't given it quickly, she would start to yell even louder. It was sort of an awkward situation, considering that we were being watched by a large handful of people throughout all of this time. The on

119

looking psychologists, orphanage workers, lawyers, and orphanage directors all watched to see how we would interact and react to Camila. If she was on the verge of a tantrum, how would we react? What would we do if she wanted something her brothers had? It was hard for us to know exactly what to do. But we continued to play and interact with Camila, often distracting her to something different if she seemed to be getting irritable with one activity.

Camila starting fussing more and more, and so I grabbed her up and began swaying and rocking her. She immediately began sucking on her middle two fingers, and lifted up the back of her shirt, grabbed my hand, and moved it back and forth on her back. She wanted me to rub her back! She quickly began dozing off in my arms. When Danny came close by, she leaned over and reached for him. She soon fell into a deep sleep on his shoulder. Danny's eyes brimmed with tears. He was finally holding his sweet little girl, his own daughter!

All at once, it was determined by the orphanage director and the SNA lawyer and psychologist that we should go on and take Camila with us for the afternoon. She seemed to adjust and interact so well with our family that they felt she could spend the afternoon with us. But shortly after, we were told she could just go ahead and stay with us for good! We were shocked, and also actually felt a little numb to the knowledge that we were bringing our daughter to stay with us after only merely knowing her for a few hours. That was not what we had expected at all! In fact, Marisa had never heard of this happening in all of her years of assisting Peruvian adoptive families.

It was a very strange scene. There were no last goodbyes or even acknowledgement from the workers that Camila was officially leaving, besides a short interaction with two British volunteers. I thought, perhaps, it was because they knew we would be coming back for the going away party. It still seemed sad to me because this orphanage had been Camila's home since she was eight months old, and there was not a single permanent worker in all of the people there who had known her all of this time, coming to bid her farewell or kiss her goodbye.

We were sent to our apartment with some final details about Camila and her care by some of the workers, along with a small bag containing the medications she was on. One of them was an anti-convulsant for seizures, one was Haldol- a major antipsychotic, and then another medication that we had not been previously informed about at all. That medication was basically a form of Valium. We were in complete astonishment! Why was our daughter, so tiny, being given all of these medicines? We never could get much of an answer. One final word of shock came from the kind volunteers who had been working at the orphanage for nearly a year. They told us that we should know that Camila had been kept in her crib all of the time, because no one could keep up with her. We were so saddened by hearing this that we asked over and over again if we were hearing correctly. It was true. We were told that she was only allowed out of her "cot" for meal times. We were so heartbroken, yet this explained so much about her difficulty interacting, staying focused, and paying attention. No doubt, the medicines must also be playing a huge role in her behaviors. We couldn't imagine why a three-year-old would be placed on these crazy medicines? But now we could see that her lack of stimulation and interaction with others must have already taken a serious effect on her social and cognitive abilities. Our poor little girl.

We were also given some clarity for the first time on why Camila was taking the medicine for epilepsy, and had been supposedly diagnosed with grand mal epilepsy. She had had three febrile seizures during her stay at the orphanage, each time being when her fever got very high while she had some sort of flu. This puzzled us because we knew febrile seizures were not a sign of epilepsy, or something that required medicine. Why then were these diagnosis in her file?

We caught a moto taxi, and it began drizzling rain outside. The moto taxis had a plastic flap on the front that could be pulled down to keep water from splashing on the driver and its passengers. I figured out that was truly something to be grateful for. Without it, a moto taxi ride wasn't exactly a dry ride. We arrived at our hotel and carried our Camila upstairs. She was still completely conked out.

It wasn't long though, until she was up, consumed with curiosity and exploring our apartment. She ran all over looking in rooms, peeking in suitcases, and standing on beds to look out of windows. She wanted to check out everything. We soon decided to take her for her first swim in the hotel pool. No doubt, she thought that was the greatest thing known to man. She kicked and splashed and was in kiddie heaven. We had to hang on tight to her though, because she was wiggling and throwing her weight constantly. One thing was for sure, she absolutely loved water!

Chapter 17

Truth in Trials

We figured out at our first meal together that Camila took food very, very seriously. In fact, she couldn't get it into her mouth fast enough. She would smash fistful after fistful into her mouth until she practically choked. If there wasn't another fistful readily available, she would begin hollering as loudly as she could in a combination holler/grunt. It was very difficult to keep her happy at the table. When you filled her cup, she immediately gulped it down until it was empty and then began hollering as loudly as she could for it to be refilled. Let's just say it made it near to impossible for mommy and daddy to eat anything. It appeared that, as long as she could see food, she would throw a tantrum to have it, even if she had already eaten plenty of her own.

It was difficult to think of why she had developed these behaviors, which are common to kids adopted from hard places. Was this a behavior that was developed from infancy when her needs weren't likely being met, or was it a behavior that had come from living in an institution where perhaps there wasn't enough food to go around? Camila was very skinny, without any excess body fat anywhere to be seen. She did, however, have very healthy looking hair. It was unclear where or why she had developed such an issue surrounding food, but it was no doubt there. And the fact that it was there was proof to us that at one point or another, she had become afraid she wouldn't be getting her next meal. Some of the food behaviors were obviously from her simply never being taught how to eat. My heart broke at all of these hard realities.

Over the next few days, I felt as though I was constantly scanning Camila, wondering where or why certain behaviors were present. It was difficult for me to know if there were some mental issues going on, or if Camila had merely suffered at the hand of being overly prescribed medicines and denied interaction, and she was now simply paying the price. I had moments of fear, when I found myself attempting to assess her actions and question the root of their nature. It was a heavy weight to bear to feel so uncertain about what was really going on with our Camila. When I felt overwhelmed, I would have to pause and fall into the arms of love again, resting in the peace of knowing that we were right in the center of God's will regardless.

Camila hid herself behind her arms a good portion of the day. She would hold one hand over her ear, and the other she would hold across her forehead and eyes. She ran all over the place like this. When she got excited, or a couple of times during a tantrum, she would take her fist and punch herself right in the back of the head. We let her know right off that this behavior would not be accepted. When she knew she was not getting the results out of us she had hoped for, she never really tried that trick again. This became a first proof to us that she was beginning to understand some of what we were teaching her.

This is also how we began to simulate, between trial and error, what behaviors Camila had gained as attempts at getting attention or had picked up due to not having social interaction. Some of these behaviors could have been due to Camila soothing herself during times when evidently she had no one around to comfort her. I wept over and over at the thought of her spending her time alone in a crib with no one to play with, talk to, and no one to love her.

Camila sucked on the two middle fingers of her right hand nearly constantly. If she was sitting still, she had those fingers in her mouth. Sometimes she walked around with them in her mouth. She had a callous on one of the fingers from it. Evidently she had been doing this for so long, and so vigorously. One day when I was brushing her teeth, I realized that she had developed some sort of callous looking blisters on the roof of her mouth from sucking so hard on her fingers all day! I had no idea that that was even possible.

The first week of our time together seemed a blur as we attempted to get to know Camila and understand the depth of her needs. We quickly learned that she was a very intelligent girl, and a fast learner. She loved for us to hold her and tickle and snuggle her. She would repeat just about anything we did, excluding words. Camila would never repeat words, no matter how hard I tried to get her to. But she repeated most other things she saw us doing. If she saw that I was laying the shoes in a row by the door of the apartment, she would grab any shoes she saw and bring them to that spot. After she saw me clean up some water spills, she wanted to clean up any mess someone had around the apartment. She was there in a flash with a rag or towel and wiping it away.

After a few days, she began to be content to sit with us for longer spells, allowing us to read or sing to her. She loved to dance, and any time music started, she was swaying back and forth with a huge grin on her face. No doubt, dancing was one of her favorite things to do, and boy did she have rhythm! We had brought a Dora movie with us, and she also adored it. She would run by the TV and kiss it when Dora was on the screen. She wasn't stingy with her sugars. She would kiss us all of the time and loved for us to hold her.

The first few nights weren't easy ones. Camila slept with us, but getting her to actually go to sleep was next to impossible. She would cry and cry and seemed mad and terrified all at once. I couldn't help but wonder what was going on in her little mind. I know she must've been so used to her routine at the orphanage, so used to life, no matter how good or bad it was. All in one day she had been ripped from everything she had ever known as stability and complete strangers had taken her away. I wondered if she thought we were another set of temporary orphanage workers that might be gone tomorrow. How long would it take for her to realize that we were here for her, and we were here to stay?

One night, as I tried and tried to console her to what seemed to be no avail, I finally resolved to take my Bible off the night stand and begin reading. I started in the Psalms and read until I came to the 23rd Psalm. I read it repeatedly until a sudden calm came over her that she had been so far from before. I laid my hands on her sweet little brown forehead and began praying. I wept as I cried out for deliverance from fear and for her to have real peace. Before my hands left her head, she was sound asleep. I knew that the Lord had brought her sweet rest that night.

At the end of the first week, on Friday morning, we had to return back to the orphanage for the going away party that was customary in Peruvian adoptions. We were unsure of how we felt about bringing Camila back to the orphanage after her being away for several days, and finally making some progress. We did not want her to regress and go back to some of the behaviors we were working hard to help her overcome.

Friday afternoon we loaded onto two moto taxis. Two liter drinks, goody bags and gifts for the orphanage caregivers, chips and cookies were all packed onto the taxis with us. Camila had on a beautiful dress and had a big cloth flower in her hair for the occasion.

Soon after we arrived, the cake was delivered, and then the music started. All of the kids came out under the large open pavilion and the boogying began. Camila seemed to think this whole arrangement was terrific. She joined in the dancing and laughing. The caregivers could not believe her behavior. They could not believe that she would even stay under the pavilion and not take off running. They were amazed to see how far she'd come in a matter of days.

Suddenly, all at once, it was as if Camila recognized some of the older children and workers who normally might have held her on occasion and attended to her. She ran to one of these girls and wanted them to hold her. When Danny and I went over to try to get her, she acted mad at us for attempting to. When everyone began eating, Camila ran to these certain people and wanted them to feed her. She would get mad if we tried to feed her and then she would run back again to these same people. The only way we could distract her, was by turning her attention to playing with us. We could hold her and dance with her, and she would be temporarily side tracked.

I felt ashamed when I realized that this was making me jealous. Why wouldn't she let us care for her? Why was she refusing our love and attention? Although she had really only known us for a few days, It still hurt to feel rejected.

Camila was certainly confused. She had been brought back to the place that she had called home now for nearly three years. Why should I expect anything different? These people were all that she had known for a long time, and I knew that it was going to take time for her to grow and trust us. Either way, it still was a strange feeling I had whirling around inside of me.

When it was time to leave the orphanage and the children began exiting the pavilion, Camila tried to take off with them and go back to her previous home. I guess she had assumed her time with us was simply a brief break from normal life, and now it was time to get on with her regular one. We happily grabbed her up, and got out of there as fast as we could.

That night Danny and I had a heart to heart about how we had felt that day at the orphanage when Camila wouldn't accept our desire to love and care for her. It had really made us both feel so helpless. In the moment, we both realized how much the scene reminded us of the way we frequently respond to Jesus' loving hands. He is constantly reaching out to us, constantly desiring to console and help us, yet we often keep running to a million other people and things to heal and help us. All when our heavenly Father is the only One who can bring about absolute restoration. He is a jealous God. He is jealous when we won't accept the blessings He has for us and we keep running to empty places for more false hope. We had

127

experienced a small bit of that same jealousy that day at the orphanage. We were jealous to love our daughter, and jealous for her to desire our love.

These sort of things happened pretty often in the early days with Camila. If we had to stop in a store for something, she would try to gain attention from anyone who walked passed by hollering or putting off a really loud, fake laugh. It could be funny at times, and it could be discouraging at other times. If she had thrown a tantrum and not received the hoped for response from it, she would reach for and try to get any stranger or passerby to grab her. She would be mad at us and want to go with someone else. Anyone else. Sometimes strangers thought this was cute, and they would attempt to take and hold her. I would hang on to her and smile and pretend I didn't know what was going on.

Winning a child's heart was turning out to be harder than I could have imagined. It obviously was not an overnight resolve. Camila was having to learn to trust us. She was having to learn that something was finally going to be constant in a life where she had been let down so often. No doubt, this would take time. Only the Lord knew just how much.

One of the first things we had to do after Camila was in our care was bring her to a doctor for a check up. This was another of those times that we were so thankful for Leslie's help. Lee Lee kept the boys while we went with Marisa to a pediatrician in Iquitos. When we arrived at the office, we found out that the doctor wasn't expected to be back for several hours. Marisa would be catching a flight out that very evening and so we didn't have several hours. We needed Marisa, because the doctor didn't speak English, and we didn't speak well enough Spanish to explain to him Camila's medications, history, and for him to explain anything at all to us, for that matter. We were learning that this was typical Iquitos living. Even though we had called to confirm we were coming to the office, the doctor still wasn't there and wouldn't be back for hours. Hilarious.

Danny and I did our best to occupy Camila in the very large and open waiting area. There were toys and games, so we took turns sitting on the floor and attempting to get Camila to focus on an activity for a few minutes at a time. We made a very scary discovery that day. In that open waiting room, the door was also wide open to the busy Iquitos street. Camila would wait until we were sitting on the floor beside her, or were on the opposite side of the door, and then she would get a big grin on her face and dash at lightening speed out of the open door towards the street. Regardless of how much we asked her to stop, she still attempted this. After that, Danny and I took turns standing guard at the doorway end of the waiting room. It was obvious that Camila had not learned any borders, and she would rush toward danger with a smile on her face. It was a tiring wait to keep her from escaping, but we did it!

Thankfully the doctor soon arrived in the nick of time, and we were able to get Camila's check up done. The doctor reviewed Camila's brain scans and the electroencephalogram that she had done. We were astounded when he told us that both brain scans were normal, and electroencephalogram did not show grand mal epilepsy, or anything at all for that matter. She was being given a strong epileptic medicine, even though the ECG clearly showed no sign of epilepsy. Even at the bottom of the test results, in Spanish, it read, "No epilepsy." We could not understand why any doctor would have written the opposite in her file. Neither could this pediatrician. The doctor also was taken aback by the medications Camila was being given. Unfortunately, he would not tell us the best way to begin weaning her off of these heavy medications. He did not feel comfortable taking her off of any of them since he would not be able to monitor her over a period of time to see how she responded. That was disappointing, considering that we would not be able to see our own pediatrician at home for around four to six weeks. It made us just as uncomfortable to continue "drugging" our daughter, which also was not helping in her ability to connect and attach with her new family.

While the pediatrician discussed these things with Marissa, I had a beautiful moment of connecting with Camila through play. I started pointing out the different parts of the face to her. I would touch her nose and say, "nose." Then I'd touch my nose and say "nose." Then I would rub our noses together and say it again. She loved this game and quickly pointed to her nose and said, "nose." It was the very first word she repeated for us.

In moments like these, when Camila seemed to really get something I was telling her, it would refresh me all over again. Any bit of progress helped me to see that things were moving forward, even if in small doses. It really was a breath of fresh air in the middle of realizing the heaviness of teaching a three-year-old little girl every little thing about living, because that was how this really was. Camila knew nothing about real danger, real living, or even how to eat or behave normally. She seemed like a baby in a three-year-old's body having so much to learn. When I thought on that, I felt beyond overwhelmed. I did my best to run back to the knowledge that we were right in the middle of where the Lord had led us, and that He was going to be with us throughout every inkling of teaching Camila, as well.

That evening I emailed some friends in the states to ask about the medicines Camila was taking. One of them was a doctor who was very familiar with Peru and the medications. He verified what we already knew in our hearts. It just was not right how Camila was being treated. We had not felt right about these medicines to begin with. Danny and I made the important decision that night to begin removing one drop of medicine from Camila every four or five days. That was the smallest dose that we were able to remove. We could not continue what we knew to be abuse. We loved Camila, and we knew that being drugged was not in her best interest. We prayed that the withdrawal symptoms would be very mild as she learned how to function without these major drugs.

The day finally arrived for Marisa, our wonderful in-country representative, to go back to Lima. She left for Lima on an evening flight, and we were left in Iquitos for our family placement week. It felt strange to be in this lively jungle city all alone, but it also felt exciting and adventurous. Thankfully, we had gotten to visit the church of our missionary friends, the Rolfzens, already. We knew that we had them if we needed anything at all, and we were looking forward to being able to see a bit of the work they were doing there in Iquitos.

Early in our family placement week, our hotel set up a tour for our family with a guide. It was one of the coolest things we had ever done as a family. We took three moto taxis to a far side of Iquitos where we walked through a waterside market. The Amazon river was overflowing into all of the surrounding rivers at that time, and it was overflowing a good bit more than normal. Everything was flooded, and so we walked on make-shift board bridges, past homes and stores that were full of water. In front of the homes, there would be kids playing and swimming in the water and women washing their clothes. We walked until we came to a small area where boats were parked along the water. There, we caught a boat.

The boat carried us to an animal reserve where the boys got to see an anaconda, along with tons of monkeys and a strange looking turtle. The monkeys hopped right passed us as we walked on more of these very narrow, make-shift bridges. The monkeys used the rails of the bridges to get around. Josiah, Isaac and Amaus thought that was great! No zoo we had visited in the States had monkeys running around on the loose! Camila, on the other hand, wasn't as impressed. She clung to us for dear life and was terrified of the monkeys. Leslie was able to hang on to Amaus, and Danny and I took shifts holding Camila and guiding Josiah and Isaac around. While there, the boys spotted a sloth in the top of one of the trees out past the bridge/walkway. Supposing the boys wanted to see it up close, the man who worked on the reserve jumped into the flood water, swam over to the tree and climbed it. He grabbed the sloth and swam back to the bridge with it. As we were getting back on the boat, the boys got to take turns holding the sloth. It was a really amazing experience for them. They found the sloth to be a very stiff animal, who was also pretty stinky. Josiah was sure it was from the algae that commonly grows on sloths because of how slow they move. Who knows, but a sloth was indeed pretty stinky.

After that we went to a butterfly garden in the Amazon jungle, and to see the Bora people, an Indian tribe who lives in the jungle and is used to associating with tourists. The Boras did a dance for us and insisted we join in. They showed us around their little village and sold us some of their handmade jewelry and carvings. Their village houses were tiny lofts on stilts that had thatched roofs. There was one kitchen that the entire village shared, which was simply another open hut with a thatched roof. Needless to say, it was an awesome day and a real blessing to be able to experience some of the Amazonian culture.

One other day that week, we took another boat ride to Belen, also called the Venice of Iquitos. All of the homes in Belen are either along the water or floating on the water for part of the year when the waters rise. We were told the people began living there because the land/water was free. Some of the homes were nothing more than what appeared to be some tin or makeshift materials all leaned up together to form a shack. Small children sat on the porches or sides of the floating homes. Many of them played in the water, and we saw several women doing their hand washing in the water. A little girl who looked about six paddled past us in a canoe as she smiled and waved.

Later that week, we learned some hard realities about Belen, and Iquitos in general. Danny had the opportunity to go out with our missionary friends the Rolfzens one night on the streets of Iquitos. The Rolfzens brought a team of Peruvian Christians, and some other missionary interns out each week late at night. They walked the streets and simply made themselves available for people who might need prayer. They themselves walked and prayed, sometimes stopping to sing and chant to the rhythm of a beat box. Danny would be forever changed by what he saw that night.

The streets were flooded with prostitutes, drug dealers and children, many of whom were dealing drugs and prostituting themselves. The police did nothing about this at all, as they seemed to be afraid of the street people of Iquitos. On the edge of Belen, was the infamous Belen market. It is known worldwide as a place where people come to smuggle and sell various jungle animals in an under-the-table black market. It is known by night as an open drug and sex market. The tables where fruit, herbs, and everything else known to man is spread abroad by day, at night is spread with a host of drugs and crowded by the addicts and homeless. Prostitution is so rampant that there are sections of town divided into what type of prostitute a buyer is seeking. There is the child prostitution area, and Belen itself is known for housing a huge market for this horrendous practice.

The Rolfzens were dealing first hand with many child prostitutes who were homeless or thrown out of their homes. Some children were forced while others chose the life of prostitution because they felt they would starve if they didn't. Young men were commonly thrown out of their homes when the mother had a new live in man who did not want to support some other man's sons. Those boys were left to fend for themselves. Girls aren't as quickly disposable since they can bring an income to the family. Many of the street kids quickly become addicted to drugs, and prostitution becomes the only means for them to support this habit. The Rolfzens were personally working with a few young men who were trying to break free from this hard past.

One of the young men confided in the Rolfzens that he was known as the gringo prostitute. And the Rolfzens became aware that people were traveling to Belen as pedophiles from all parts of the world to participate in the terrible trade of prostitution in Iquitos. Because cocaine could be purchased on the streets for around ten cents, children became addicted, and soon were trapped into the street life, doing whatever it took to support their habit.

Danny saw for himself that night that the problem of drugs and prostitution was huge. His heart was broken for these people who had become known as the street people of Iquitos. Many of them longed for a better life, but saw no window of hope or even a small chance of escape.

One afternoon, Danny, Leslie, the kids and I took a couple of moto taxis to visit the Rolfzens. They walked us down the road to a home they called the Safe house, where they were housing around forty men who had come off of the streets and had made the decision to break free from the life of bondage they had known before. Some of these guys had been delivered from addictions for nearly a year and were now leading other men to Jesus. They had a heart like no other for the people they knew who were still trapped in drugs and prostitution.

The Rolfzens saw a great need for a home for children and women. They were also currently renting a house for two prostitutes who had made a vow of purity, along with their children. These women were turning away from the hurt and bondage of their pasts and working to earn money to provide for themselves and their kids. The rented home was a make-shift for the much greater need, a need for a larger women and children's home. It became a need that Danny and I also became burdened for that week in Iquitos.

I was able to go out with a team to the Belen market early one morning where the street people are given bread to eat. Many of them are still asleep on the market tables and barely look alive after a night of drug binges. These addicts gather around to listen to the team sing to the beat box rhythms. The team prays for these people and then they are given bread to eat. It is an amazing opportunity for many of the Safehouse guys to minister to their old friends and show them that there is a better life for them in Christ. I, too, was brought to a state of real brokenness at the sight of so many people in need.

It made my heart turn to our precious Camila, who would have undoubtedly been driven to a life like this had we not have responded to the cry we had heard so clearly two years before. But what about all of these kids? When was their deliverance to come?

Our two visits with the psychologist that were required for the family placement week went very well. Camila displayed to the psychologist what she had been showing us each day, more and more; that she was attaching to us well. She also played non-stop. Her favorite things were a set of stacking cups that I had brought with us from home. She stacked and re-stacked the set of ten cups, seemingly never getting bored of it.

She also adored balloons and would throw and catch them for hours on end.

We noticed very little change in Camila after we removed the first drop of medication, other than her ability to sleep at night seemed disrupted for about three days. We continued to pray over her each day, and her behavior got a tiny bit better.

That Thursday Leslie finally had to leave and go home to Louisiana. We were so sad to see her go. I knew that God had placed those extra hands with us for the first part of our time in Peru, and I have no idea what we would have done without her. She truly helped us immeasurably. Les flew out of the small Iquitos airport to Lima. Our good friends, the Lamonts kindly took care of her for the day in Lima and had her back at the airport late that night to catch her flight to the states.

On the following Monday, because of the psychologist's reports being favorable, we were able to go to the SNA office of Peru and sign the papers that made our adoption final. We were officially Camila's parents. What a huge relief it was for it to finally be official.

Marisa arrived back in Iquitos that Tuesday evening to help us take care of getting Camila's new birth certificate on Wednesday morning. This was a routine part of the process. A new Peruvian birth certificate had to be issued, with Camila's new parents and new name on it. That was required for her to obtain a passport and visa to leave the country.

Tuesday was a legally required "day of silence," which gave anyone wanting to protest the adoption a chance to speak up. If no one did, the adoption was official on Wednesday morning. As was typical, the adoption was not contested and became final Wednesday morning! Camila was officially our daughter!

Marisa had been warned that the Reniac, the government office who handled issuing new birth certificates, would tell us that it would take 30 days to obtain a new birth certificate. However, that was simply the amount of time that it normally took, and for an international adoption, it would be rushed through much faster. Sure enough, when she arrived at the Reniac to apply for the new birth certificate, she was given the typical 30 day expected wait. Marisa, who was our wonderful advocate, insisted that it could not take thirty days. She pleaded that we had already been in Peru for nearing three weeks, and we could not stay for another thirty days. The response she received was not what we had expected. She was told by the Reniac that they did not have the program they needed at the time to cancel out Camila's old birth certificate in the computer system that they were now changing over to. They had to cancel out the old birth certificate before hey could issue a new one. Then came the even more unbelievable ticker. They would not be getting that needed computer program, the one for canceling out birth certificates, until the end of the next week. Even then, the birth certificate could not be issued until, more than likely, the beginning to middle of the week after they got the new program.

When Marisa brought us the news in our upstairs apartment, we had no idea what to do. Danny was set to fly home from Lima with our boys the following Monday, which was only a few days away. All along we had planned on flying to Lima on Friday evening. It was quickly looking like Camila and I would be in Peru for an additional two weeks, and that was an optimistic estimate.

Apparently, this problem with obtaining birth certificates in a speedy fashion was a new problem for adoption from Peru. Up until the previous few months, a new birth certificate could be written up in a day or two by the judge in each province. Now that the birth certificates had to be obtained from the Reniac, it was causing some extra red tape to be dealt with. This new red tape that had caught us entirely off guard.

That night in our apartment, Marisa helped us to figure out a plan so that Camila and I could be back in Lima after Danny left for home. We all felt better about me staying with the Ardiles for any of our extra wait, rather than Camila and I having to hang out in an apartment alone in Iquitos.

The only way to work that out was by us signing over power of attorney to allow someone in Iquitos to sign Camila's birth certificate when it became ready. Then that person would have to air mail it to Lima where we could get it. Our missionary friends, the Rolfzens were willing to do that for us.

The next day we waited for a few hours at a notary in Iquitos to have the power of attorney written up. Trent and his friend Rudolpho both were given an extremely long list of things to remember to do dealing with the birth certificate, on our behalf. I honestly felt terrible asking them to do these things. And while I knew they were very trustworthy men, it left me feeling uneasy to leave all of this unfinished business in Iquitos. I knew we could only hang on for these things to be tied up, while we waited in Lima. We didn't know what else to do, though. It was either Camila and I wait in Iquitos alone, or wait in Lima with the Ardiles'. The latter of the two options became our final decision.

Thankfully, we were able to get a flight out of Iquitos the next evening. It was a Thursday. We had one last, delicious Iquitos breakfast at our hotel, and we began packing up our belongings. Everything had become quite settled on that 3rd floor apartment. We had been living there for a few days shy of three weeks now. It felt strange to now be rushing out in a hurry. Danny and I agreed that day, as we rolled up clothing, souvenirs, and toys and packed them away in our stack of luggage, that is was undoubtedly a very mournful feeling we had to be preparing to bid farewell to the vibrant jungle city of Iquitos. It had touched our hearts in a way we had not prepared ourselves for. We knew we would never be the same.

Josiah, Isaac and Amaus were very ready to be going home to their country home that allotted them the freedom to run and play outdoors at their will. It had been hard for them not to have anywhere to romp and explore, like they were so used to doing every day. Camila, on the other hand, seemed very confused by our speedy packing. She followed us around fussing and crying all day long. It was as if we were packing up all the joys she had discovered in the previous few weeks, and she couldn't figure out why. I wondered if she thought we were bringing her back to the orphanage. After all, our temporary apartment was probably what she had assumed to be her new home.

We were able to break away that afternoon, fitting our entire family of six into one moto taxi. We looked like we were in a clown car! We road out to say goodbye to our friends the Rolfzens. We enjoyed one last good visit (and a good cup of coffee) with this amazing family of believers. They prayed for Camila, and our family, and we said some final teary goodbyes before we caught a moto taxi back to our apartment.

That evening the kind hotel bell boys came up to get all of our luggage and load it into the hotel van. We crowded into the van, which was a crazy feeling after not riding in an automobile for so long. The van air conditioner was blasting, and an American radio station played some eighties hits. We had gotten so adjusted to Iquitos living that actually riding in an air conditioned vehicle with music felt bizarre. Immediately, Camila began to reach up to the ceiling of the van and her eyes got extremely wide. She began breathing very heavily and was turning her head in all directions to look around in awe of the van.

That's when it dawned on us! Camila had never ridden in a vehicle before! She had only left the orphanage to go to the doctor a few times, and that had undoubtedly been in a moto taxi. She was completely star struck on the entire ride to the airport. The old eighties love song came on..."We've got tonight. Who needs tomorrow?" and Camila began throwing her voice high and low when the male and female parts changed. It was pretty funny. She apparently thought riding in this "bubble" with AC and music entertainment was pretty swell!

As we drove across Iquitos to the airport, I looked over at Danny, who had tears pouring down his cheeks. I didn't need to ask him why. It was surely a sad feeling to be leaving Iquitos.

It felt like we were leaving another home. The people of Iquitos had struck a chord in our hearts. We couldn't possibly leave Iquitos unaffected by all that we had experienced and known there. It felt like we were leaving unfinished business, and we both were saddened by if and when we would be able to go back.

By the time we arrived at the airport, Camila was in a less than pleasant mood. The packing of the day, the first car ride, all of it amounted to way too much stimulation for a little girl who had scarcely left the walls of an orphanage in her short life. By the time we got in line to check our bags, the fight began. Camila was obviously terrified. I kept going back to the thought that she might be having some fear we were about to leave her. After all, everything she had come to know as routine with us was being thrown out the window, and in a hurry! She began fighting to get out of my arms, hollering and crying. It was a serious struggle. When I wouldn't let her down, she began hitting me in the face. We were certainly the spectacle of the Iquitos airport. I'm sure the scene looked something similar to a kidnapping. I could not seem to find anything to bring Camila peace.

After checking our bags, we had to wait in another line where our passports and Camila's paperwork would be checked. This was a bit nerve wracking considering the fact that we didn't actually have Camila's birth certificate yet. When we finally made it to the front of this line we were sent by the officer back to a police station in the airport. Danny and the boys were able to go on through to the place where they'd board the flight. Camila, Marisa, and I went back to the station. Camila was still hollering loudly and fighting me to get down. I sat, exhausted in an empty chair in the small office where Marisa discussed our paperwork with the police officer. Camila suddenly reached out towards a jug of water beside a desk in the office and began hollering, "Abwa-Abwa!"

That was the very first time Camila had vocalized any word to us while asking for something. The police officer quickly offered Camila some water. She bottomed out the cup of water in typical fashion, and began throwing a tantrum for another cup. By now, the police officer and Marissa were busy looking over our papers and I didn't feel like I could interrupt. It was a trying few minutes as Camila threw an all out tantrum right there in the office, and I couldn't seem to gain control for the life of me. It was all I could do to not melt to a million pieces right there on the spot. My face was quickly turning red and I could feel the hot tears gathering in my eyes. I bit my lip to hang on to my emotions, and my little girl.

Finally, we were cleared to go back and made it through that final security point to sit where Danny and the boys waited. I knew Camila was in desperate need of a diaper change. I rushed her to the bathroom to try and wash her face and get her a clean diaper. She became more afraid in the bathroom and continued to scream. She was terrified of the hand dryer and screamed and stiffened her body in complete fear. We got out of the bathroom as quickly as we could.

As we boarded the flight for Iquitos, Camila calmed down a bit. Soon though, that ended when she realized she couldn't get down, and she had to sit in a seat with her belt buckled. She screamed and cried and threw her body weight. I tried holding her, but she wouldn't let me. It was a very, very difficult moment. All of the people in the seats around us just stared. I wondered why they wouldn't just look away for a minute. I felt bad for them because I'm sure they were wishing they'd taken the earlier flight. I felt bad for me because I didn't really care to be the entertainment for the flight to Lima.

Things didn't get much better. When the flight attendants brought a small meal, it was only a temporary distraction. The screaming and crying picked right back up. When we finally landed in Lima, I looked down to see that Camila had been biting one of her nails to the point of making it bleed. Our poor daughter was just so afraid.

On the taxi ride from the airport, Camila finally crashed. I nearly did. We arrived to what felt like home when we drove to the Ardiles' home late that night. Their sweet and welcoming faces were a real ray of sunshine to the worn out travelers. We all slept like babes that night, with the city sounds and the open windowed breezes blowing in once again.

We spent the weekend being treated to more wonderful Peruvian cooking and the Ardiles' hospitality, and living in deliberate ignorance of the fact that Danny and the boys would be leaving on Monday night. It was too dreadful a thought, especially without any knowledge of when Camila and I would be able to leave. We pretended it wasn't coming and tried to enjoy the weekend.

Monday night came quickly though, and before I knew it, a taxi arrived to pick up Danny, Josiah, Isaac and Amaus. I helped them load their bags into the taxi, and I cried huge tears as I saw the taxi drive to the end of the Ardiles' road and turn off. It was the loneliest feeling in the world for my husband and three sons to be leaving, and for me to not have any inkling of an idea of when I'd be able to join them.

Chapter 18

Walking Through the Valley

I walked into the Ardiles' tiled entryway, stepped onto the first step of shiny wood, leaned against the wall and sobbed my eyes out. I couldn't get it together, no matter how hard I tried. Señora Ardiles came and reached up to me. Her petite frame only came to my shoulders, but she put her dainty arms around me and hugged me. Fiorella came and translated as Señora Ardiles spoke to me the words of wisdom that a woman who had walked with the Lord for many years could say with confidence.

"We have to trust that God has a reason for having you here. We have to trust and have joy that Jesus will bring about His will. We cannot worry, but we must trust. God will take care of Danny and Josiah, Isaac and Amaus. He will take care of you and Camila, too."

I knew she was right. I was trying to absorb the words, but I was so very sad that it was hard to. I hadn't expected to be so sad. I had known that I would probably be staying on an extra week in Peru without Danny and the boys. What I had not known, was that extra week might turn into two or more weeks. That really seemed like an eternity to me.

Señor and Señora Ardiles did their best to keep me busy that week of supposedly waiting for the Reniac to get the computer program they needed to print Camila's birth certificate. It was a week where nothing required for our process could be accomplished. All that we could do was wait. The Lamonts teamed up on the efforts to keep me encouraged and busy. I don't know what I would have done without all of them that week.

One day Señor Ardiles took a taxi with me where a friend of Anita's lived, and she let us borrow a stroller. That was a beautiful thing to have! We walked around a park and caught another taxi to a mall. Señor Ardiles was the kindest gentleman, following me around the mall and carrying my bags for me. It was the sweetest thing ever. Señora Ardiles and I went to another huge mall two times that week and walked around laughing and visiting. Camila had become a pro at shopping malls. She acted Ike a queen riding around in the stroller. If she was given a drink of her own, you'd think she had been given the greatest gift in the world. She would ride around as content as could be, taking in the sights.

I made a couple of Starbucks runs with Fiorella that week, and we made a stop at the Indian market, which was incredible. I could have spent all week there! There were things brought in from all over Peru that were handmade at different regions of the country; Some of it right there in Lima. There were so many beautiful things. I was able to get some really cool authentic Peruvian gifts to bring home for friends and family, and save for Camila, as well.

During the daytime of that week of waiting, Camila and I spent a lot of our time playing together in the upstairs sunroom. It was the one area that I could close off and she couldn't take off running. We played games, danced and repeated the same games. We read books, sang songs, and ate snacks. We did whatever we could to pass the time.

Since I knew that Camila and I would be having lots of one-on-one time that week, I decided to really focus on teaching her to use the potty. I knew I wouldn't be able to focus so much undivided attention on her when I got home. She already would use the potty on occasion, but also used her diaper most of the day. By watching her, I could tell that she really knew when she needed to potty. I began taking her to the bathroom frequently, and from the very beginning, she only had a couple of accidents a day.

Each night at bedtime, we had developed a little routine of me reading her the 23 Psalm, reading her a story, and praying for her. She seemed to love those moments at night, and so did I. She would drift off to peaceful sleep, and I would finally call Danny to discuss with him the day's happenings and how much I missed him and the boys. It broke my heart to speak to them. At the end of the first week, I couldn't talk to the boys without weeping, and it was all I could do to hold it together for a short conversation.

Trent and Rudolpho had been busy working on our behalf in Iquitos. They had gone to the Reniac nearly every day asking how they could speed up the process of getting Camila's new birth certificate. At the end of the week, they were told what we had thought all along, that they had had the program they needed to cancel out old birth certificates all along, and that was merely just something Marisa had been told to brush off the ability to issue a birth certificate speedily. I was very upset when I got that word. After all, I had been sitting around all week for no reason at all, and I could have been on my way home by now. That hurt.

On Monday, I felt desperate. Trent and Rudolpho could get no answers at the Reniac. Marisa began calling people she knew in Iquitos who might help us. Every one would say they were willing to help, but nothing would happen.

Each morning in Lima, Marisa and I would go to the local Reniac and see if the birth certificate was ready. Each day we would be sent home without a birth certificate. A birth certificate would show up in the computer system for Camila, but it didn't have the official seal that was supposedly required for it to be printed. The workers at the Reniac said they couldn't print it until it had that seal. We were told it would take about a week for that seal to show up in the computer system.

Tuesday evening, after making several calls to various officials at the Reniac, Marisa was told by a director at the Reniac that the birth certificate was just as official without that seal, and that the Reniac in downtown Lima could print that version for us. The birth certificate was what we needed to get the passport. The passport was what we needed to get the visa. All three were required to leave the country and go home.

We rushed to downtown Lima the next morning, which was a Wednesday, and after chasing a few rabbits, finally had several copies of the "extract of the birth certificate" as they called it, in hand! We rushed to the passport office, took Camila's passport photo, and waited in another line for about an hour. I was filled with such joy. I knew I would be going home.

A few minutes later, we were called to the back office, where the director of the passport office informed us that we could not, in fact, get a passport with only the extract of the birth certificate. That the passport office had its own laws to follow, and it could not give us the passport until we had the birth certificate with the actual seal. What disappointment! I hoped and hoped we would be able to convince the director, and she would help us. She wouldn't. That was that.

Marisa had been able to get us an appointment with the US Embassy doctor for that Wednesday evening. It was one thing we could get done with or without the birth certificate. It turned out to be a very emotional visit, after a very emotional day. Camila was scared to death at the office. Once we finally got into the back exam room with the doctor, Camila started acting very strangely. It seemed that more of the questionable behavioral issues that we had been seeing dissolve each day, always came out when she was scared or nervous. One of those behaviors, where she would look off into space and put this fake grin on her face, usually came out when someone wanted her undivided attention and she became nervous. Camila did that constantly that night while the embassy doctor watched her. Before we left the office, the doctor essentially told us that she believed that many of Camila's behaviors were probably from the medications and the lack of stimulation, but that she believed that she had some kind of neurological damage. That wasn't what any mom wants to hear. As if that wasn't bad enough, Camila was given four required shots before we were able to step outside and stroll around for a minute. I had to get out of that office. I had to have some air.

The doctor's office was right beside a monastery. I remember hearing the music from a mass coming out into the street, and smelling the smell of incense burning. All I could do was walk and weep, and cry out to God to deliver me and bring us home. I was overwhelmed by the doctor's words. Was this doctor right about our daughter? I did not want to believe the doctor. I did not want to be in Peru anymore. I cried out to the Lord as I walked around outside of that monastery. I cried out for God to move and bring me home.

I went back to the Ardiles' that evening ready to burst. When was I going to be able to go home? It was nearing the end of my fifth week in Peru, and we still were searching for answers and information about when we would have Camila's birth certificate in our hands. At our regular supper where we usually enjoyed a cup of coffee and chabata bread with Señora Ardiles and Fiorella, I had another break down. The buckets of tears fell at the kitchen table. I told them all about what the doctor had said and how I wanted so desperately to finally know when I'd be going home. I couldn't take the not knowing any more. I needed to be home with my husband and sons!

Señora Ardiles had words of comfort for me once again. She encouraged me to read Psalm 23, and she hugged me. She urged me to continue to trust that the Lord knew best. She did not know that Psalm 23 was what I had been reading to Camila each night as I prayed for God to remove her fears and give her peace. God wanted me to read it. It was for me, too. He wanted to remove *my* fears and give *me* peace. I knew I needed it.

That evening as I dwelled on Psalm 23, I saw so clearly what I had been needing to see for days. That night I blogged:

"I have decided something. You know how you get to the end of yourself from time to time; you finally tell your flesh to, "Shut up," and you choose to trust again? Well, if you're human, you know! Sometimes you don't even mean to begin to doubt, but circumstances are opposing your desires and so you start. Whatever the cause or reason, big or small, we always come out with greater joy and greater victory when we simply trust.

That's it. I have decided to trust. Many, many people are praying. We are surrendered to God's will for our lives. Can Satan do something in the life of a surrendered believer that God has not allowed? Absolutely not. Therefore, I have decided to rest in knowing that my God is moving and bringing about His plan at the perfect time, and no opposing power can stop that.

Trusting brings so much more joy than unbelief. I choose joy. I choose joy even if it means I must stay in Peru for three more weeks. After all, I am still just the clay, here. Sometimes I need to be broken down a little (or completely), so Jesus can make something more useful. I'm thankful that my King delights in using this vessel. Since He created it- He surely knows what's best for it.

I have been reading Psalm 23 to Camila most nights. She seems to really look forward to the time when I'll lie beside her with only the bedside lamp and read the scriptures to her. She sucks on those two little fingers and grins at the same time. It's precious.

I went to bed last night rejoicing that I would be leaving Peru. I read the Psalm to Camila, and after she was asleep, I came downstairs and blogged about my joy.

This morning things didn't go as planned. I came back to the Ardiles' home, and Señora Ardiles began to encourage me

150

to rest in the Lord and His timing. Then she took a slip of paper and wrote 'Salm 23' (Psalm 23) on it. She wanted me to read it. She didn't know that that was the chapter I've been reading every day to Camila...but God wanted to give it to me.

I love how the Lord works. It's as if God is telling me to trust His leading (the essence of Psalm 23), when the news is good, as it was just last night, and when it's not so good.

Psalm 23
The LORD is my shepherd;
I have all that I need. He lets me rest in green meadows;
he leads me beside peaceful streams. He renews my strength.
He guides me along right paths,
bringing honor to his name. Even when I walk
through the darkest valley,
I will not be afraid,
for you are close beside me.
Your rod and your staff
protect and comfort me. You prepare a feast for me
in the presence of my enemies.
You honor me by anointing my head with oil.
My cup overflows with blessings. Surely your goodness and
unfailing love will pursue me
all the days of my life,
and I will live in the house of the LORD
forever

I know that my Shepherd is leading me in RIGHT paths for HIS namesake. But right after that, it says: 'though I walk through the darkest valley, (or the valley of the shadow of death) I will fear no evil. For you are with me. Your rod and your staff, they comfort me.'

Sometimes the Shepherd leads us into darker valleys. It might simply be a place or circumstance, or DELAY, we don't prefer. It's still the Shepherd leading, though. Don't be fooled into believing there won't be hard days when you follow the great Shepherd. Jesus told us that, 'No servant is greater than his master.' Jesus, the Son of man, had no place to lay His head. So you better believe we will face trials and dark valleys in this life! BUT... His rod and staff, they are a comfort to us. He doesn't lead us into a dark valley and then say, "Alright! Fend for yourselves, sheep! See ya later!" No. He's with us. He's with me; comforting me in the night, and teaching me of His faithfulness. He brings defeat over my enemy. He fills my cup with blessing until it overflows! He anoints my head with oil (sets me apart for His purpose)!

What do I lack with the great Shepherd? Absolutely nothing at all. Even when I'm far from home. Even when my hands are tied. Even when I long to hold my sons and hug my husband. Even then. I can trust that He is also holding up all of the other sheep involved, as well.

I didn't have that comfort before I knew Jesus. I led myself into dark valleys and chose to hang out there without a protector. But once I trusted Jesus Christ, I never have had to fear again. Sure, I've chosen fear at times. But thankfully, after a bit, I feel a nudging at my shoulder. Yes, it's my Shepherd gently tapping me with His staff. He's reminding me that He is the One who led me here, and He'll be the One who leads me out in due time."

That night the word of God brought me peace once again. After Camila was settled in bed, I finally was able to talk to Danny on the phone. Danny had determined earlier in the week that if we did not have the birth certificate in hand by Wednesday, he was coming back to Lima. It was Wednesday, and we had no birth certificate. So that evening, he had actually booked his flight to leave for Lima early Thursday morning. I couldn't believe it! God provided the money for his flight, and he was coming back to be with me. Truthfully, there was absolutely nothing he could do to bring about this birth certificate any faster, but the thought of him being with me was an amazing comfort. I could not wait to hug him! Early the next morning, practically in the middle of the night, Danny would be flying back to Lima. I wouldn't see him until the following night around midnight, but I was beyond excited!

Señor Ardiles had friends who worked at the Reniac in Lima, and they were also advocating on our behalf to see that the birth certificate got to Lima, and quickly. Anita had a friend who worked with the Reniac in Iquitos, and they were also advocating for us. What else could be done? We prayed and stood that the birth certificate would be issued any day now.

The next morning, Thursday, we rose early and went to the Reniac once again, just as we had been doing for nearly a week. Marisa hoped that they might possibly have issued the ID card by now, which the passport office considered equivalent to a birth certificate. With the ID card we could still get the passport and the visa. We were disappointed to find out that the ID card had not been issued. But at the very last minute, as I was preparing to leave, Marisa rushed over to tell me that, while the ID card wasn't ready, the official birth certificate finally was! We could print it off immediately and rush to the passport office!! I thought about jumping up in the middle of the Reniac and dancing a jig!

That was the best news of my life! Of course, it was also very hilarious. Danny was now on an airplane on his way to Lima! He had no idea that we would have the birth certificates, passport, and everything needed to turn around and leave in a matter of twenty-four hours! What news he would have upon arriving in Lima! Hopefully, if everything went well, we could probably fly home the following night. Oh, the irony.

We were able to get Camila's passport without a hitch. Marisa was also able to set up our embassy appointment for that same day! That was our final hoop to jump before being able to fly out of Lima. She brought us back to the Ardiles' where we had some lunch, and Camila took a short nap.

That evening we went to our final required appointment in Peru with the US Embassy. They had already meticulously combed over Camila's file months back, but we were required to have one final interview and scan of her information before her visa could be issued. The interview lasted about an hour and was very simple. Basically, after we left the office, the computer system was able to scan her picture, and every picture worldwide in a missing children's photo database to be sure that Camila might not be a child missing from anywhere in the world. This was customary for any internationally adopted child. I thought that was pretty amazing. If all of the scans came back clear, the visa would be ready the following afternoon. Wow. We were finally going home!

Chapter 19

Sweet Resolve

Late that night a taxi arrived with my dear husband. We held each other for what seemed like forever. It brought me such comfort to see him. He really couldn't believe it when I told him that the birth certificate had been issued that very day! "Oh well," he said. "I did what I thought I needed to."

He brought me a bag of chocolate Easter candy that I thoroughly enjoyed for a few hours! I was just closing up the Hershey's and Cadbury Eggs bag of goodness at midnight. It was my first bit of chocolate in five weeks, and man was it good!

The next day, Friday, was busy. Danny got on the phone first thing that morning and started trying to book our flight home for the evening. Unfortunately, he hit wall after wall. He was told there were no seats available, and then next he was told that if we wanted to fly out before Wednesday, it would cost us an extra three thousand dollars. Wednesday? "Please no!" I prayed to myself. I also got others praying back home.

We asked the Lord to make a way for us to fly home that very evening. We needed to get home to our sons, and we didn't have three thousand dollars available to do it. We asked God to work a miracle and bring us home.

After three hours on the phone with United Airlines, a lady began working to help us out. When she found out our flights were involving adoption and that we had been in Peru for five weeks, she did all she could to help us. We were able to get a flight home that evening, and the fee for changing our flight from its previous scheduled time was only about $1500! Astounding. That was close to exactly what we had remaining in our adoption account. Our God is a precise God!

That afternoon we made one final trip into town to Miraflores and to the Indian Market with Fiorella. We met Anita and Angus there and were able to give them a hug goodbye. What kind-hearted people. We rushed back to the Ardiles', finished packing quickly, jumped in the shower and got downstairs in just enough time to share some last minute tears and words with the Ardiles household.

Danny couldn't find the words to express his gratitude for the Ardiles' willingness to help us, and the comfort it was to him that Camila and I were in good hands when he had to go home. His tears and choppy words came out muffled, but I know they heard his heart loud and clear. I felt so happy to be going home, but I sincerely felt like I was leaving family as I hugged them all goodbye. They had been the hands and feet of Jesus to me over the last two weeks. I'm not sure what I would have done if I would have been stuck in an apartment all alone for that two weeks, bearing the weight of loneliness and fear without any comforting words to steer me back on track. It had been tough. I knew that the Lord had used them in such a mighty way and I felt forever indebted to them for their love and unending hospitality to our entire family. They had shown us the true love that brothers and sisters in Christ should share and display worldwide. What a standard they had set!

With weepy eyes we rushed into Marisa's car. The Ardiles' waved to us until we drove away. We were bidding fare-well to our Peruvian family.

The flight home was seamless. Camila slept for most of it, and I did my best in typical awkward fashion, laying my head on the metal arm rest, on the tray table...anywhere, in hopes of catching some shut-eye on the seven hour flight to the United States.

Upon stepping onto US soil, Camila became a US citizen by way of being adopted by two US citizens. Arriving in Houston merely felt like it was around the corner from home.

The adventure of bringing our daughter home was at an end. After two long years, and the greatest struggle of faith of a lifetime, we finally held a promise fulfilled in our arms. God directed us each step of the way. We had never seen the Lord move like we had witnessed over that two years of waiting, learning, and standing in faith.

As we held our little girl, we knew she was just the one that the Lord had led us to several years earlier. I had to wonder where she was when I had dreamed of being in a muddy river in South America. Was she on the street crying for someone to attend to her, and had the Lord awakened me up to her cry so many thousands of miles away?

I suppose I'll never know that until I get to heaven. One thing I do know, the Lord proved to us time and time again, that He desires to direct and lead the lives of His children to unknown places, if they'll only listen and believe Him.

I knew the real adventure was only beginning; the beginning of healing, and the beginning of watching God's plans for Camila unfold. This truly was only a point of setting sail for the longer journey lying before us. But if Jesus had taught us anything through the process of adoption, it was that He would never leave us alone. Not then, and not now. The same God who began this work of deliverance would bring it to completion. That was a fact, and we would stand on it in faith.

Chapter 20

Learning To Love The Early Days Home

The early days at home were filled with lots of learning opportunities for our entire family. Danny and I were gradually understanding the boundaries and limitations Camila needed to help her grow and learn. The boys were learning what it was like to have a sister. Camila was learning what it was like to have a whole lot of attention, guidance, and opportunity to be a little girl who could run and play and explore.

She immediately thrived in ways we never could have imagined. As soon as we got home, she began repeating words we would ask her to. Shortly after, she began asking for things, "Agua, outside, daddy..." More came from her little mouth weekly. She began saying please and thank you, and she began telling us every time she needed to go to the bathroom. She replaced hollering with words.

She was soon off all medications that she had been prescribed, and more of the true Camila began to shine. She became focused, attentive, and her intelligence became progressively clearer and clearer. Her eyes had a new, curious sparkle in them. Camila woke each morning with the sun and ran from one end of our home to the other end in absolute glee. She adored her room and playing with toys. She loved playing chase and being outside. She thought our fluffy cat Rosa was the funniest thing in the world.

Over the early months, certain behaviors that had puzzled us began to dissolve. She hid behind her arm less and less. She stopped sucking her fingers, and completely quit looking off into space nervously. Some of those behaviors first disappeared at home, but would still come out in public places. But in time they dissolved no matter where we went.

Camila began learning borders. She would not try to run away from us and would even walk calmly beside us without us even holding her hand. She would follow instructions, clean up her toys, and participate in games. She slowly began interacting with other kids and attempting to join in whatever activity they were playing. It was astounding to watch her progress.

We quickly learned certain places and environments that she was not yet comfortable with, and we spent the early months primarily at home.

There were times when other well meaning people would not understand the things we were trying to do to teach Camila about life, family, and trust. At first we would try to explain to these people why we had to be so consistent and so attentive, but we eventually found that people still really couldn't wrap their brains around our reasonings. So we stopped explaining and just kept doing what we knew to be best. There were times when people would not respect the borders we desperately needed to set for our daughter, who was learning how to trust her mommy and daddy. During those times, we would have to be firm and put our foot down. We knew it didn't really matter if the world at large disagreed or misunderstood our attempts to teach Camila, we had to do what was best.

Some of those things revolved around the bonding process. She needed to bond and attach to her mama and daddy before other relatives and friends, and in the early months it was not important for people who would not be a consistent part of her life to come around once every six months and attempt to get her to fall in love with them. That would only hinder the permanency we were working tirelessly to teach her- the fact that we were going to love her, and we were there to stay.

Some of the other issues revolved around certain things that Camila had never been taught, such as the fact that she could not run to and take food from anyone's plate that she saw, and that there is a stopping point in eating and drinking. Those things were very challenging for a while, because many people unknowingly assume that if a child begs for food, they must be hungry or thirsty. This was not always the case with Camila, who could have just finished an entire plate or two of food and several cups of drink, and would still beg for or take food from people. For a while, she would literally eat until she threw up if we let her eat as much she asked. After we knew Camila had eaten enough, people would often continue to give her food, at times against our wishes. It was difficult for us to teach her the concept that there is a stopping point, and that she couldn't take food from others' plates when people would continue this. We had to be firm, or just completely avoid those situations until this became something that Camila understood. Bit by bit, day by day, she began to understand more that there would be enough food for her at the next meal.

Our entire family adored Camila. They fell in love with our little bundle of excitement and personality, and we grew in our love for her each day. We were really learning to love in a way that we had never thought possible. This kind of love required us a degree of patience we had never required in parenting our biological children. This kind of love challenged us to respond to trials and situations in the attitude of Christ and not with the way that we felt. It beckoned us to stop looking at what we physically saw before us and instead stand on the knowledge that the Lord had victory in mind. He alone would bring it to pass. It was a calling to a dependency on Jesus that we had never afforded in our day in day out living, previously.

Camila began seeing doctors upon our arrival at home. Our pediatrician, like many others, said there would be no way to know overnight if Camila's delays were merely from her previous environment or from something deeper. Time began to prove, however, that Camila was perfectly fine. We brought her to an incredible pediatric neurologist who reviewed her brain scans and also found no problem whatsoever. She assured us that she could see no reason to put Camila through the trauma of further testing unless we had a reason, and she could see none. Camila simply was not the same child that we met that first day at the orphanage.

Camila began physical, speech and occupational therapy. We were already working at home on most of the things she was doing at therapy. But nonetheless, her progress was amazing.

Our family had another surprise when we arrived home from Peru. Exactly one week from when we flew into the Houston airport, I began to notice that something wasn't quite right with me. I decided to take a pregnancy test, and sure enough, I was pregnant!

The timing of this event was certainly divine. It had been about six months since we had surrendered our family size to the Lord. Had I gotten pregnant even two months sooner, our adoption would have been completely stopped. But God had it all under control, all of the time. We had never suspected at any time while we were in Peru that I might be pregnant. What a crazy thing to be home for one week and find out a new baby would be arriving! Only the Lord could orchestrate these things! Undoubtedly, the Lord was showing us once again that He is worthy to be trusted with all matters in our lives, and if we allowed Him to do the leading, there would be no end to the miracles.

As I've seen Camila change, I've seen changes come to pass within myself. In moments of impatience and tiredness, I am reminded that God is the One who will ultimately take care of every situation, and all of my strivings won't. There is still a sifting going on in me. A long needed sifting away of my selfishness and an unrelenting passion to be the hands and feet of Jesus in my very household, is the necessity. One day at a time, one month at a time, I have been able to weigh the pureness of my surrender. Many days I find myself on my knees crying out to God for help. Many days I feel so far away from where I want to be. "Help me to really love the way you love, Lord Jesus," is my daily prayer.

In all of the adventures of the last two and a half years of our family life, God has made it so blatantly clear to us. It's the same simple message He whispered to my heart nearly four years ago in the form of a dream of a muddy river in South America.

"If you will only surrender to Me, I will use you in a way you never could have imagined."

This has become the anthem of our household. Day in, day out, we desire to pour ourselves out to the One who poured Himself out for us. Day by day, we want to surrender everything before Him. Our dreams, fears, our finances, our expectations. Because we know that God never intended for His children to sit idly on the sofa of contentment in a picket fence life that never requires giving, trusting or brokenness.

But as we have had the joy of seeing so vividly firsthand through the handiwork of the great King of Kings Himself, the surrendered life is the only life where true joy, unsurpassing peace, and amazing victory resonate loud and clear. It's in this place of surrender where the world sees the light of the Father shine through with absolute radiance. It's where we learn to trust. It's a place we never want to leave.

The proceeds from the sale of this book go to support the work of Trent and Shawn Rolfzen in Iquitos, Peru. Abundant Life Ministries currently has a "Safehouse" for men that have come out of the drug scenes. They are in the process of building The Jessica House for the prostitutes and orphans on the streets of Iquitos.

Abundant Life Ministries for Peru is a non-denominational ministry in Iquitos, Peru, founded by missionaries Bruce & Gail Unterschuetz. Trent & Shawn Rolfzen, along with their six children, began their adventure in Iquitos in October 2009. They are actively reaching out to the beautiful people of Iquitos and surrounding areas by hosting Kid's Camps, Kids Clubs, and city wide outreaches.

Giving:
Abundant Life Ministries for Peru
6010 Meadowbrook Road
Benton Harbor, MI 49022
Attn: Trent and Shawn Rolfzen

Mailing:
Abundant Life Ministries for Peru
Apdo. 732
Iquitos, Peru

To give online go to: www.newcreationwoc.org
Click on World Missions and find Trent and Shawn Rolfzen

20585485R00089

Made in the USA
Charleston, SC
18 July 2013